All rights reserved. No part of this publication
may be transmitted or reproduced in any form
or by any means without prior permission
from the publisher.

ISBN: 978932130427

Recipes © Sonal Ved
Food photographs © Karam Puri

Editors: Nicole Mody, Neelam Narula & Isha Maniar
Design: Sneha Pamneja
Pre-press: Jyoti Dey
Production: Lavinia Rao

Photo Credits: Alamy (Pages 8-9, 16-17, 18-19, 22-23, 90-91,
179, 181, 182-183, 185); Getty Images (Pages 6-7);
Karam Puri (Pages 144-145, 164-165, 176-177, back cover)
Illustrations: iStock

Published by Roli Books in 2023
M-75, Greater Kailash II Market
New Delhi-110 048, India
Phone: ++91-11-4068 2000
Email: info@rolibooks.com
Website: www.rolibooks.com

Printed and bound at
Naveen Printers, New Delhi

INDIA LOCAL

CLASSIC STREET FOOD RECIPES

SONAL VED

FOOD PHOTOGRAPHY BY
KARAM PURI

Lustre Press
Roli Books

CONTENTS

CLASSIC CHAATS FROM INDIA

Faraal Sev Puri 24
Geeli Bhel 25
Classic Sev Puri 26
Sukha Bhel 28
Dahi Bhalle 30
Dahi Gujiya 31
Dahi Papdi Chaat 32
Dhakai Chaat 33
Sukha Puri with Aloo 34
Surti Corn Chaat 34
Paneer Dahi Vada 36
Karari Aloo Tikki Chaat with Peas Filling 38
Creamy Aloo Chaat 40
Alu Kachalu 41
Bomb Batata 42
Chinese Bhel 44

Kolhapuri Bhadang Chaat 46
Bihari Chaat 47
Bihari Ghugni 48
Amritsari Bun Chaat 49
Rajasthani Mirchi Vada 50
Banarasi Tamatar Chaat 52
Indore Namkeen Chaat 53
Cheeseling Bhel 53
Vitamin Bhel 54
Healthy Moth Ki Chaat 56
Sweet Potato Tikki Chaat 57
Tulsi-Cinnamon Fruit Chaat 58
Peanut Chaat 58
Kala Chana Chaat 60
Kulle Ki Chaat 61
Tawa Paneer Chaat 62

Raj Kachori 64
Pyaaz Ki Kachori 66
Chole Chaat 67
Tokri Chaat 68
Samosa Chaat 70
Ragda Patties 71
Fafda Chaat 72
Palak Patta Chaat 73
Kanji Vada 74
Ram Ladoo 76
Nimki Makha 77
Jacket Potato Chaat 78
Kand Tikki Chaat 80
Karari Bhindi Chaat 81
Pani Puri 82
Chicken Chaat 84
Crispy Lamb Bhel 86

STREET FOODS OF INDIA

Sindhi Dal Pakwan 92
Manipuri Singju 94
Butter Sada Dosa 94
Jinni Dosa 96
Kothambir Vadi 97
Lal Aloo Wai Wai 98
Daulat Ki Chaat 100
Bun Maska 100
Bohri Samosa 101
Indori Kees 102
Cutting Chai 102
Mango Lassi 104
Kashmiri Kahwa 104
Shikanji 105
Aam Panna 105
Jil Jil Jigarthanda 106
Thukpa 106

Frankie 108
Thair Vadais 109
Amritsari Kulfa 110
Kashmiri Masalah Tchot 112
Khopra Pattice 114
Sel Roti 114
Bombay Pav Bhaji 115
Kanda Bhajiya 116
Railway Cutlet 116
Amritsari Macchi 118
Sundal 118
Atho 120
Mountain Maggi 120
Vada Pav 122
Tender Coconut Shake 123

Dakor Na Gota 123
Bombay Sandwich 124
Paneer Tikka 126
Kumaoni Bada 126
Kolkata Kathi Roll 127
Kashmiri Mutton Tujj 128
Paknam 130
Egg Banjo 131
Egg Tikka 132
Bhindi Bazaar Seekh Kebab 134
Chicken Shawarma 136
Mutton Momos 137
Sha Phaley 138
Muttai Kalaki 140
Bihari Kebab 140
Keema Baida Roti 141

UNIQUE CHAATS FROM MY KITCHEN

Cheesy Paneer Cone Chaat 146
Pani Puri with Asian Slaw and Fragrant Herb Water 148
Barley and Couscous Tikki, Mango Cream and Birista 149

Papdi 'Lasagna' with Orange Yoghurt 150
Quinoa and Olive Tikki Chaat 152
Burrata Papdi Chaat 154
Ragda-Khari 156

8-Layered Dhokla Chaat 157
Tuscan Kale Chaat 158
Avocado Taco Chaat 160
Guacamole Galauti 160

CHAAT MASALA, CHUTNEYS & DIPS

Chaat Masala 166
Chaat Masala 2 166
Chaat Masala 3 167
Kala Chaat Masala 167
Mint–Coriander Chutney 168
Date–Tamarind Chutney 168
Green Chilli–Garlic Chutney 169

Tamarind–Jaggery Chutney 169
Red Garlic Chutney 170
Green Chilli–Coriander Chutney 170
Sesame Seed Chutney 171
Lemon Chutney 171
Momo Chutney 172
Kashmiri Doon Chetin 172

Mullangi Thuvaiyal (Radish Chutney) 173
Besan Chutney 173
Papdi 174
Guacamole 174
Palak Chutney 175
Spicy Green Chilli and Peanut Chutney 175

Legends of India 178
Glossary 186
Index 190

INTRODUCTION

For me, it is no coincidence that the word 'chaat' rhymes with 'heart'. Right from the living rooms on Altamount Road and the weddings at Umaid Bhawan Palace to the chaotic streets of Old Delhi, chaat is an omnipotent category of dishes (food group, if you may please), the sheer accessibility of which binds people together, no matter what their social or economic status. A ubiquitous part of the collective Indian culinary identity, irrespective of background, of region, of affordability, the love for chaat is similar to a religion that suits everyone: you don't like the spiciness of teekha pani puri, let the sweet potato tikki chaat soothe your palate. You don't like the zero-textured dahi vada, let the crunchy papdi chaat rescue you. Unable to get the kids (and some adults) to eat their fruits and veggies? In comes my original recipe, vitamin bhel. Truly, the road to our hearts is paved with chaat *thelas*.

However, the most debated aspect of chaat isn't Mumbai versus Delhi (of course Delhi wins). It is the origin of it. According to one story, when Emperor Shah Jahan fell ill, a royal hakim advised him to eat food loaded with spices to strengthen his immunity. The palace *khansama* came up with chaat, a dish that was light on the stomach but tasty at the same time. There is another legend from the same period about a canal (perhaps the River Yamuna) supplying water to the local homes becoming polluted, because of which the court hakim advised the locals to cook using a lot of healing herbs and spices like tamarind, coriander, and mint. I believe that these are just tales, since some version of dahi vada can be traced all the way to *Manasollasa*, an early twelfth-century Sanskrit text composed by the Kalyani

Chalukya (the Kannadiga dynasty is sometimes referred to as Kalyani Chalukya), in which King Someshvara III shares much socio-cultural information that gives us a view into the Chalukya dynasty's culinary life. This scripture mentions the existence of dishes that combined vadas, purikas (similar to the puris of pani puris or papadis), curd, and a variety of spices. Though chaats may have become well defined during the Mughal period, they existed in various forms earlier too.

Each street food has its own unique story of origin. A dish called sundal finds a mention in literature dating to the Chola period. One of the references mentions the Chola royals snacking on roasted peanuts with a sprinkling of fresh coconut, similar to sundal sold commonly in Tamil Nadu even today – sundal is the first snack I grab when I visit Chennai. The railway cutlet and railway mutton curry originated during the British Raj. The British did not want to eat kebabs with their hands, so locals in Kolkata (then Calcutta) innovated to roll the meat up in a paratha and the kathi roll was born. Chinese bhel, a snack made of chutneys and fried noodles is an illustration of Indo-Chinese exchange, which traces back to Hakka Chinese traders who settled in Calcutta in the late 1700s when it was the capital of the British Empire in India, while the Bombay sandwich is said to have originated to feed the migrant workers who thronged the city during the mill industry boom in the 1960s. In 1967, Indian hockey player Amarjit Singh Tibb visited Beirut. On his return he introduced an Indian inspiration of the shawarma known as the 'frankie' (named after the West Indies cricketer Frank Worrell). The first Tibb's Frankie opened in Mumbai in 1969, and there has been no looking back for the franchise ever since with its legacy spanning fifty-three years over 160 outlets.

Today, however, each Indian state has its own interpretation of these dishes.

There is an ongoing debate that questions if all chaat is the same as street food. The answer is simple – *all chaat is street food, but not all street food is chaat.* For example, a Bombay sandwich or a Bihari kebab is street food, but it isn't chaat. But pani puri is considered street food and chaat at the same time. Street food can most certainly be a replacement for a meal, something that fills your stomach on a busy day. But chaat, chaat is made of moments when that puri breaks apart as you try to bite into it, and a medley of flavours explode on your tongue and remind you of when you climbed up trees on hot summer days to pluck imli pods and eat it.

The well-travelled gourmand, chef Anthony Bourdain, once said, 'I've long believed that good food, good eating, is all about risk.' A study into the migration patterns of those hailing from Uttar Pradesh is a true testament to Bourdain's words. The early migrant, who ventured into the northern and western states of the country in the twentieth century in search of livelihood, was ready to take a risk as he put up his *thela* to sell the variety of chaats he grew up eating. And that begs the question – why did the geographical distribution of chaat follow an almost set course? Was it because it was easy to return and bring home the wealth gained from selling age-old flavours to the city folk? It surely makes one think. Talking about geographies, while writing this book, one truth about chaats and street food that glared right at me is that one can find the former abundantly in North, central, East and West India, while southern India has little to no chaats on their regional menu. It is perhaps the extreme hot or cold climate of the North and West that made them want to reach out for a hot plate of aloo tikki or a cooling bowl of papdi chaat accompanied by a tall glass of lassi in the by-lanes of Mathura. While South is where you'll find ample street food, from deep-fried vadais, podi-splattered dosas, parotta to porichathu and bondas. Additionally, dairy, which comprises yoghurt, is a big part of chaats and is not as widely used in the South as much as in North India. In fact, according to historians, North Indians and Western Indians consume far more milk and milk products than East Indians or South Indians and it has to do with a certain gene mutation which allowed the North Indians to digest milk better than the Southerners.

Besides favourite chaats and street foods such as sukha and geeli bhel, dahi bhalle, peanut chaat, frankie, kanda bhajiya, vada pav, Maggi noodles, and paneer tikka, this book also delves deeper to bring to fore some lesser-known dishes like the Burmese atho from Chennai, Darjeeling's laal aloo Wai Wai, Sikkim's sel roti, Indore's egg banjo, Uttarakhand's Kumaoni badas and much more.

And if you think those are unique, I cannot wait for you to browse through the section titled 'unique chaats from my kitchen'. Here, I've shared recipes that were born not in the sun-kissed streets of Lucknow or the noisy alleys of *purani Dilli*, but in my Gujarati home. My family is obsessed with chaats and we don't repeat recipes often, which leaves me with only one option – to come up with unique ways to transport those flavourful chutneys, crispy papadis and sev into my mouth. Pick from a creamy burrata papdi chaat that

I learnt from one of India's best chefs, Manish Mehrotra of Indian Accent fame, an avocado taco chaat I created for a Diwali party, the quinoa and olive tikki to keep it friendly with health-conscious friends, a kale chaat that tastes good only when made with Tuscan kale versus curly kale and so much more.

The book also has recipes from a few renowned Indian chefs such as Prateek Sadhu, Saransh Goila and Hussain Shahzad who were generous enough to teach me a recipe or two for my cooking show 'Chaats of India', and a loaded section featuring the best Indian chaat and street food eateries across India.

Enjoy this journey, because I surely have.

CLASSIC CHAATS FROM INDIA

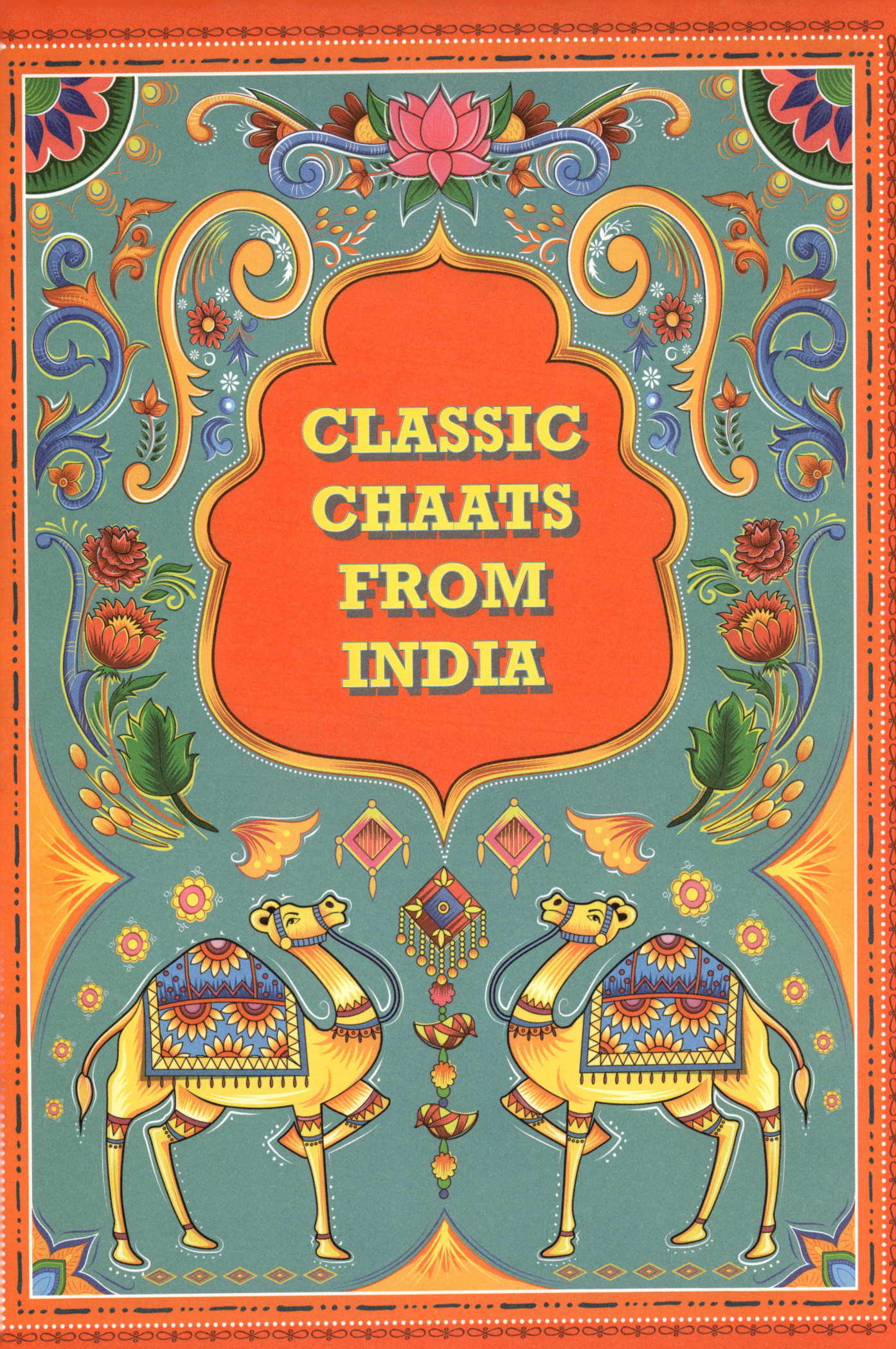

MAHARASHTRA

Faraal Sev Puri

Millet and amaranth flour crisps topped with chutneys

Time taken: 30 minutes | Serves 4

Ingredients

FOR THE CRISPS/PAPDI
1 cup amaranth flour
½ cup barnyard millet flour
1 teaspoon cumin seeds, roasted, slightly crushed
1 teaspoon salt
1 tablespoon vegetable oil
Water to bind
Sunflower or any neutral oil for frying

FOR THE TOPPING
¼ cup yoghurt
1 teaspoon powdered sugar
1 cup boiled and finely cubed potato
¼ cup boiled and finely cubed sweet potato
2 tablespoons finely chopped coriander leaves
1 teaspoon chaat masala (page 166)
Salt, to taste
Date–tamarind chutney, to taste (page 168)
Green chilli–coriander chutney, to taste (page 170)
3 tablespoons pomegranate gems
1 cup yoghurt
Sev

Method

1. **To make the crisps/papdi,** mix the flours and crushed cumin seeds together in a bowl. Add a teaspoon of salt, a tablespoon of vegetable oil and combine with your fingertips.
2. Add water, a few teaspoons at a time, and knead until you get a tight, shiny dough. Divide the dough into 5 or 6 parts and roll them into large rotis. Meanwhile, heat the oil in a kadhai over medium heat.
3. Pierce tiny holes onto each roti with a fork and cut them into smaller rounds using a circular cookie cutter (1½ to 2 inches). These are your papdis.
4. Deep fry the papdi in hot oil until golden brown. Use a slotted spoon and drain on kitchen towels until they come to room temperature.
5. While the papdis are resting, whisk the yoghurt with powdered sugar until smooth.
6. **To assemble** the chaat, mix the cubed potato, sweet potato, chopped coriander leaves, chaat masala and salt in a bowl. Toss well until evenly coated. Divide the mixture between the papdis and add dollops of both chutneys. A spoonful of yoghurt topped with pomegranate gems and sev is the perfect finisher.

📍 MAHARASHTRA

Geeli Bhel

Mixed snack of puffed rice, sev, vegetables, and chutneys

Time taken: 10 minutes | Serves 4

Ingredients
1 cup toasted puffed rice
1 tablespoon masala peanuts (available at grocery stores)
1 tablespoon masala chana (available at grocery stores)
1 tablespoon spicy chana dal (available at grocery stores)
1 large kachori, crushed (page 66)
2 tablespoons boiled and finely chopped potato
2 tablespoons finely chopped onion
2 tablespoons finely chopped tomato
1 tablespoon finely chopped raw mango
1 teaspoon red garlic chutney (page 170)
½ tablespoon green chilli–coriander chutney (page 170)
1 tablespoon date–tamarind chutney (page 168)
¼ cup nylon sev
2 papdis, crushed (page 174)
1 tablespoon chaat masala (page 166)
1 tablespoon lemon juice
2 tablespoons finely chopped coriander leaves

Method
1. Place the puffed rice in a big bowl and top it with masala peanuts, masala chana, spicy chana dal, kachori pieces, potatoes, onions, tomatoes, and raw mango. Toss well to combine.
2. Add the chutneys one at a time, followed by nylon sev, crushed papdi, chaat masala and lemon juice, stirring frequently to distribute evenly.
3. Garnish with coriander leaves and serve at room temperature.

◉ MAHARASHTRA

Classic Sev Puri

Crispy shells topped with potato mixture, spices, and chutneys

Time taken: 10 minutes | Serves 4

Ingredients
10 papdis (page 174)
¼ cup boiled and mashed potato
¼ cup finely chopped onion
¼ cup finely chopped tomato
¼ cup finely chopped raw mango
¼ cup red garlic chutney (page 170)
¼ cup green chilli–garlic chutney (page 169)
¼ cup date-tamarind chutney (page 168)
¼ cup nylon sev
5 tablespoons spicy chana dal (available at grocery stores)

FOR THE SPICE MIX
1 tablespoon chaat masala (page 166)
1 tablespoon roasted cumin powder
1 tablespoon red chilli powder

FOR THE GARNISH
2 tablespoons finely chopped coriander leaves
1 lemon, halved

Method
1. In a small bowl, combine the chaat masala, cumin and red chilli powders; set aside.
2. Arrange the papdi on a large plate and top each with a spoonful of mashed potato. Add the chopped onion, tomato, and raw mango.
3. Carefully layer the chutneys, starting with the red garlic followed by the green chilli–garlic and finishing with the date-tamarind chutney. Scatter the tops with the nylon sev and spicy chana dal, and sprinkle with the prepared spice mix.
4. Garnish the sev puri with coriander leaves and a squeeze of lemon juice before serving.

CLASSIC CHAATS FROM INDIA 27

⦿ MAHARASHTRA

Sukha Bhel

A toss up of puffed rice, sev and potato mixture

Time taken: 15 minutes | Serves 4

Ingredients

FOR THE CHUTNEY

5 spicy green chillies, roughly chopped
5 mild green chillies, roughly chopped
3 teaspoons lemon juice
2 tablespoons roasted gram flour
½ cup roughly chopped coriander leaves
1 teaspoon roasted cumin powder
1 teaspoon peeled and roughly chopped ginger
1 pinch dry mango powder
Salt, to taste

1 cup toasted puffed rice
1 tablespoon masala peanuts (available at grocery stores)
1 tablespoon masala chana (available at grocery stores)
1 tablespoon spicy chana dal (available at grocery stores)
1 large kachori, crushed (page 66)
2 tablespoons boiled and finely chopped potato
2 tablespoons finely chopped onion
2 tablespoons finely chopped tomato
1 tablespoon finely chopped raw mango
2 teaspoons sukha chutney
2 papdis, crushed (page 174)
¼ cup nylon sev
1 tablespoon chaat masala (page 166)
1 tablespoon lemon juice
2 tablespoons finely chopped coriander leaves

Method

1. **To make the sukha chutney**, place the green chillies, lemon juice, gram flour, coriander leaves, cumin powder, ginger, mango powder, and salt in a mixer-grinder and grind into a rough powder. Add a few drops of water very carefully and only if needed to adjust consistency. The final chutney should be a dry-coarse mixture that clumps slightly.
2. In a large bowl, combine the puffed rice, masala peanuts, masala chana, spicy chana dal, kachori pieces, potatoes, onions, tomatoes, and raw mango.
3. Add the prepared sukha chutney, crushed papdi, nylon sev, chaat masala and lemon juice. Toss the ingredients and garnish with fresh coriander leaves before serving.

CLASSIC CHAATS FROM INDIA 29

MAHARASHTRA

Dahi Bhalle

Lentil fritters topped with yoghurt and chutneys

Time taken: 30 minutes + 2 hours resting | Serves 4

Ingredients

FOR THE VADAS
1 cup split black gram, soaked overnight
½ cup split skinned green gram, soaked overnight
1½ teaspoon cumin seeds
1 green chilli, finely chopped
1 teaspoon chilli–ginger paste
1 tablespoon finely chopped cashew nuts
1 tablespoon small green raisins
Salt, to taste
Sunflower or any neutral oil for frying

FOR THE GARNISH
1 cup yoghurt
1 tablespoon powdered sugar
¼ cup green chilli–coriander chutney (page 170)
¼ tablespoon tamarind–jaggery chutney (page 169)
Black salt, to taste
¼ cup finely chopped coriander leaves

FOR THE SPICE MIX
1 tablespoon chaat masala (page 166)
1 tablespoon roasted cumin powder
1 tablespoon red chilli powder

Method

1. Whisk the yoghurt with powdered sugar until smooth and refrigerate for at least two hours.
2. In a small bowl, combine the chaat masala, cumin and red chilli powders; set aside.
3. **To make the vadas**, drain the split black and green grams and grind them into a thick and smooth paste, using as little water as possible. Add the cumin seeds, chopped green chilli, chilli–ginger paste, cashew nuts, and raisins. Combine well and season to taste with salt. Set aside.
4. Heat the oil in a kadhai over medium heat. Working in batches, drop spoonsful of the prepared batter into the hot oil and fry until the vadas are lightly golden. Use a slotted spoon and drain on kitchen towels.
5. Put the vadas into a bowl of water at room temperature to soak for 2 to 3 minutes. Gently press the water out of each vada and transfer them to a plate.
6. **To serve,** pour the chilled yoghurt over the vadas followed by dollops of chilli–coriander chutney and tamarind–jaggery chutney. Sprinkle with the prepared spice mix and finish with a pinch of black salt and coriander leaves.

📍 MAHARASHTRA

Dahi Gujiya

Lentil fritters stuffed with spices and topped with yoghurt

Time taken: 2 hours | Serves 4

Ingredients

FOR THE GUJIYA
1 cup split black gram, soaked overnight
Salt, to taste
3 tablespoons finely chopped cashew nuts
2 tablespoons finely chopped green raisins
2 tablespoons desiccated coconut
Sunflower or any neutral oil for frying

1 cup yoghurt
½ tablespoon powdered sugar
1 tablespoon cumin seeds
¼ cup tamarind–jaggery chutney (page 169)
¼ tablespoon green chilli–coriander chutney (page 170)
1 teaspoon roasted cumin powder
1 teaspoon red chilli powder
1 teaspoon chaat masala (page 166)

Method

1. Drain the soaked lentils and pat dry with a kitchen towel. Let the lentils rest for a few minutes. In a mixer-grinder, grind the lentils into a thick paste but do not use any water. Season to taste with salt and whisk once more. Set aside and allow it to ferment for 1 hour.
2. In a small bowl combine the cashew nuts, raisins, and desiccated coconut. Set aside.
3. Whisk the yoghurt with powdered sugar until smooth. Set aside until needed.
4. Lay a plastic sheet on the kitchen counter and ladle 2 spoonsful of the fermented batter on the sheet – you are looking for a thick circle of lentil paste. Neaten the circles with the back of a spoon if needed.
5. Gently place a teaspoon of mixed cashew nuts, raisins, and coconut in the centre of the circles and carefully fold the plastic sheet in half, forming a crescent underneath.
6. Heat the oil in a deep pan over low heat.
7. With delicate hands, open the plastic sheet and lift the gujiyas. Sprinkle cumin seeds on one side and deep fry them over low heat. The gujiyas will not break if the batter is absolutely dry and thick. Once golden, using a slotted spoon transfer the gujiyas directly to a bowl of water and allow them to rest for 4 to 5 minutes.
8. Squeeze the water out of the gujiyas right before serving. Place the gujiyas on a plate and drizzle with sweetened yoghurt, both chutneys, roasted cumin and red chilli powders, and chaat masala.

◉ MAHARASHTRA

Dahi Papdi Chaat

Crispy flour chips topped with potato, yoghurt, and chutney

Time taken: 30 minutes + 2 hours resting | Serves 2-3

Ingredients
1 cup yoghurt
3 teaspoons powdered sugar
¼ cup tamarind–jaggery chutney (page 169)
10 papdis (page 174)
¼ cup chunks potatoes
1 tablespoon boiled yellow peas (optional)
¼ green chilli–coriander chutney (page 170)
5 teaspoon red garlic chutney (page 170)
2 tablespoons pomegranate gems
¼ cup nylon sev
2 teaspoons chaat masala (page 166)
1 pinch roasted cumin powder
1 pinch red chilli powder
1 tablespoon finely chopped coriander leaves

Method
1. Whisk the yoghurt with powdered sugar until smooth and refrigerate for at least two hours before using.
2. Dilute the tamarind–jaggery chutney with ½ a tablespoon of water in a shallow bowl. Using your fingers, dip each papdi into this mixture and place them in a bowl, crushing gently into large pieces.
3. **To serve**, top the crushed papdi with potatoes, yellow peas (if using), chilli–coriander chutney, red garlic chutney, sweetened yoghurt, pomegranate gems, and nylon sev. You can tailor the sweetness of this dish by adding a little more tamarind–jaggery chutney.
4. Garnish with a sprinkle of chaat masala, roasted cumin powder, red chilli powder, and fresh coriander leaves.

◉ DHAKA INSPIRED

Dhakai Chaat

Layered flour-based paratha topped with potatoes, sprouts, yoghurt and chutneys

Time taken: 1 hours 45 minutes | Serves 4

Ingredients

1 cup refined flour
2 cups semolina
1 cup + 2 tablespoons rice flour
¼ cup ghee
Sunflower or any neutral oil for frying
Salt, to taste

FOR THE TOPPING
1 cup boiled and finely chopped potato
1 cup boiled sprouts
2 cups yoghurt
½ cup tamarind–jaggery chutney (page 169)
¼ cup green chilli–coriander chutney (page 170)
1 tablespoon roasted cumin powder
1 tablespoon coriander powder
1 tablespoon red chilli powder
1 tablespoon chaat masala (page 166)
1 tablespoon pomegranate gems
¼ cup finely chopped coriander leaves
Sev for garnish
1 tablespoon black salt

Method

1. Sift the refined flour into a bowl with semolina and rice flour and knead it into a tight dough using very little water. Divide the dough into 10 to 12 equal rounds and roll into pedas. Flatten each peda with a rolling pin and apply ghee on both sides. Dust with more rice flour.
2. Cut a straight line from one side to the centre with a knife. Roll it into a cone, rolling inwards from the cut, as if making a rose. Press the outer part of the cone inwards with your finger, making rose-shaped flat pedas. Keep the cones covered with a moist cloth for an hour.
3. Heat the oil in a deep pan over medium heat. Just before frying, grease your palms with a little ghee and gently flatten the pedas some more.
4. Deep fry the pedas in hot oil. Use a long-handled spoon and carefully pour a little hot oil into the centres of the 'flowers'. This will help them 'bloom'. Fry until golden-brown and drain on kitchen towels.
5. **To assemble the chaat**, place these 'flowers' on a serving plate and cover with potatoes, sprouts, and yoghurt. Drizzle over both chutneys, roasted cumin, coriander and red chilli powders, and chaat masala. Garnish with pomegranate gems, coriander leaves, and sev. Finish with a dash of black salt.

BY CHEF AMNINDER SANDHU

CLASSIC CHAATS FROM INDIA

MAHARASHTRA

Sukha Puri with Aloo

Hollowed crispy shells topped with dry-spiced potato

Time taken: 10 minutes | Serves 2-3

Ingredients
10 pani puri shells (page 82)
½ cup boiled and mashed potato
1 teaspoon red chilli powder
1 teaspoon roasted cumin powder
1 pinch black salt
1 teaspoon chaat masala (page 166)
2 teaspoons lemon juice
1 tablespoon finely chopped coriander leaves
3 tablespoons nylon sev
2 tablespoons pomegranate gems

Method
1. Gently crack a hole into the tops of the shells with your finger and place them on a serving plate.
2. In a bowl, combine the mashed potato with red chilli and roasted cumin powders, black salt, chaat masala, lemon juice, and coriander leaves. Mix thoroughly.
3. Stuff the potato mix into the waiting puris and garnish with nylon sev and pomegranate gems.
4. Serve at room temperature.

GUJARAT

Surti Corn Chaat

Corn kernels tossed with spices and cheese

Time taken: 10 minutes | Serves 2

Ingredients
1 cup boiled corn kernels
1 tablespoon melted butter
1 cup finely chopped tomato
1 cup finely chopped onion
1 green chilli, finely chopped
1 teaspoon chaat masala (page 166)
1 teaspoon powdered sugar
1 tablespoon red chilli powder
1 teaspoon cumin powder
Salt, to taste
1 teaspoon chilli sauce of choice
1 tablespoon finely chopped spring onion
1 tablespoon finely chopped coriander leaves
1 tablespoon sev
1 tablespoon grated cheese

Method
1. Place the corn in a serving bowl and top with melted butter, tomato, onion, and green chilli. Toss well.
2. Add the chaat masala, powdered sugar, and red chilli and cumin powders into the corn. Season to taste with salt. Add a teaspoon of chilli sauce and toss once more.
3. Finish with spring onion, coriander leaves, sev, and grated cheese. This chaat can be served warm or cold.

CLASSIC CHAATS FROM INDIA 35

UTTAR PRADESH

Paneer Dahi Vada

Cottage cheese fritters topped with yoghurt and chutneys

Time taken: 30 minutes | Serves 4

Ingredients
1 cup grated cottage cheese
2 potatoes, boiled and grated
1 tablespoon corn flour
1 tablespoon roughly chopped green chilli
1 tablespoon finely chopped coriander leaves
Salt, to taste
Sunflower or any neutral oil for frying
¼ cup yoghurt
½ tablespoon sugar
½ cup tamarind–jaggery chutney (page 169)
½ cup green chilli–coriander chutney (page 170)
1 teaspoon roasted cumin powder
1 teaspoon red chilli powder
1 tablespoon chaat masala (page 166)

Method
1. In a large bowl, combine the cottage cheese with grated potato, corn flour, green chilli, and coriander leaves. Season to taste with salt and create a single 'dough'. Scoop some of the mash with a large ladle and roll into dahi-vada-like patties.
2. Heat the oil in a kadhai over medium heat.
3. Reduce the heat and in batches, deep fry the vadas until they are golden brown. The lower heat will allow them to cook on the inside without burning. Use a slotted spoon and drain on kitchen towels.
4. While vadas are usually soaked in water after being fried, we are plating these straight away.
5. Start by whisking the yoghurt with sugar until smooth. Place the vadas on a serving plate and drizzle with the sweetened yoghurt, followed by the chutneys. Sprinkle cumin and red chilli powders over the chutneys and top with some chaat masala.

CLASSIC CHAATS FROM INDIA   37

UTTAR PRADESH

Karari Aloo Tikki Chaat with Peas Filling

Potato fritters stuffed with pea fillings, topped with chutneys

Time taken: 40 minutes | Serves 4

Ingredients

FOR THE PEA MIXTURE
1 tablespoon sunflower oil
1 teaspoon cumin seeds
1 tablespoon minced ginger-chilli
1 cup boiled green peas
2 teaspoons chaat masala (page 166)
½ teaspoon dry mango powder
1 teaspoon red chilli powder
3 teaspoons fennel powder
2 teaspoons coriander powder
2 teaspoons roasted cumin powder
Salt, to taste
1 teaspoon sugar
Juice of ½ lemon

FOR THE ALOO TIKKI
2 cups boiled and grated potato
Salt, to taste
1 tablespoon corn flour
Sunflower or any neutral oil for frying

FOR THE CHAAT
¼ cup red garlic chutney (page 170)
¼ cup green chilli–garlic chutney (page 169)
¼ cup date–tamarind chutney (page 168)
1 cup yoghurt (optional)
¼ cup finely chopped onion
¼ cup nylon sev
1 teaspoon chaat masala (page 166)
2 tablespoons finely chopped coriander leaves

Method

1. Heat 1 tablespoon oil in a deep pan over medium heat and add cumin seeds. Once the seeds begin to crackle add the minced ginger–chilli paste. Sauté for a few minutes before adding the boiled green peas.
2. Stir in the chaat masala, dry mango, red chilli, fennel, coriander, and roasted cumin powders and cook for another 4 to 5 minutes. Season to taste with salt and add sugar before coarsely mashing the peas. Add a squeeze of lemon juice and set aside.
3. Toss the grated potato in a bowl with salt to taste and a tablespoon of corn flour. Roll a spoonful into a ball and flatten with your fingertips.
4. Place a small scoop of the prepared mashed peas in the centre of the flattened potato. Gently push closed until it is covered from all sides, before rolling it into a ball with the pea mixture in the centre.
5. Heat the oil in another deep pan/skillet over medium heat. Carefully flatten each ball into a thin tikki and deep fry until golden brown. Drain on a kitchen towel for a few minutes. Use the back of a flat spoon and press down on the tikkis to make them thinner. Deep fry them once more to get them crispier.
6. **To plate the chaat**, drizzle the hot tikkis with generous dollops of red garlic chutney, green chilli–garlic chutney, date–tamarind chutney, and yoghurt (if using), followed by finely chopped onions, and nylon sev. Finish with chaat masala and fresh coriander leaves.

CLASSIC CHAATS FROM INDIA 39

NORTH INDIA

Creamy Aloo Chaat

Creamy potatoes with grilled vegetables and chutneys

Time taken: 40 minutes | Serves 4

Ingredients

2 cups baby potatoes, halved and deep fried
1 teaspoon tandoori masala (available at grocery stores)
1 teaspoon salt
1 teaspoon lemon juice
1 tablespoon butter
1 cup thickly diced tomato
1 cup thickly diced capsicum
1 cup thickly diced onion

FOR THE DRESSING
1 tablespoon ginger–garlic paste
½ tablespoon chaat masala (page 166)
1 teaspoon garam masala
1 tablespoon red chilli powder
1 tablespoon coriander powder
1 teaspoon roasted cumin powder
1 teaspoon dry mango powder
1 teaspoon black salt
1 teaspoon dried fenugreek leaves
1 tablespoon tandoori masala
1 teaspoon honey
2 teaspoons chickpea flour
½ cup hung curd
1 teaspoon lemon juice

FOR THE GARNISH
½ cup sliced onion
1 tablespoon julienned ginger
1 green chilli, finely chopped
1 tablespoon fresh whisked cream
1 tablespoon pomegranate gems
½ tablespoon chaat masala (page 166)
½ tablespoon finely chopped mint leaves
½ tablespoon finely chopped coriander leaves

Method

1. Toss the fried potatoes with 1 teaspoon tandoori masala, salt, and lemon juice in a bowl and set aside.
2. In another bowl, whisk together the ginger–garlic paste and chaat and garam masalas, followed by red chilli, coriander, roasted cumin and dry mango powders, black salt, dried fenugreek leaves, tandoori masala, honey, and chickpea flour. Add the hung curd and lemon juice and whisk until smooth. Set aside for 15 minutes.
3. Meanwhile, heat the butter on a grill pan over low heat. Thread the diced tomatoes, capsicum and onions alternately on wooden skewers and grill them until they are well-charred, about 8 to 10 minutes over medium heat.
4. Remove the grilled vegetables from each skewer and transfer them to a bowl. Add the fried potatoes, followed by sliced onions, ginger, and green chilli. Toss well.
5. Add the whisked cream and toss again. Finish with pomegranate gems, chaat masala, mint, and coriander leaves.

UTTAR PRADESH

Alu Kachalu

Potatoes and sweet potatoes, generously spiced

Time taken: 20 minutes | Serves 4

Ingredients
Sunflower or any neutral oil for frying
1 cup cubed potato
1 cup cubed sweet potato
1 tablespoon coriander seeds
2 dry red Kashmiri chillies

SPICE MIX
1 tablespoon coriander seeds
1 teaspoon chaat masala (page 166)
2 teaspoons roasted cumin powder
½ teaspoon red chilli powder
Juice of ½ lemon
Black salt, to taste
1 teaspoon julienned ginger, soaked in lemon juice for 20 minutes
1 tablespoon coriander leaves

Method
1. Heat the oil in a heavy-bottomed pan over medium heat and shallow fry the potato and sweet potato cubes. Use a slotted spoon and drain on kitchen towels.
2. In another small pan over low heat, dry roast the coriander seeds and red chillies until fragrant. In a mixer-grinder, grind into a coarse powder and toss with the potato and sweet potato.
3. Put the spiced potatoes into a shallow bowl and sprinkle generously with chaat masala and cumin and red chilli powders, followed by a squeeze of lemon juice. Season to taste with black salt. Toss once again.
4. Garnish with ginger soaked in lemon juice and coriander leaves, and serve.

MAHARASHTRA

Bomb Batata

A cousin of jacket potatoes, tossed with spices

Time taken: 25 minutes | Serves 2

Ingredients

FOR THE CHAAT MASALA 3
¼ cup cumin seeds
½ cup coriander seeds
1 teaspoon vegetable oil
1 cup boriya chillies
½ teaspoon citric acid
1 teaspoon black salt
½ teaspoon table salt

2 potatoes, boiled and halved
1 tablespoon butter
½ cup sliced tomato
½ cup green chilli–coriander chutney (page 170)
¼ cup green chilli–garlic chutney (page 169)
¼ cup date–tamarind chutney (page 168)
¼ cup finely chopped onion
2 teaspoons finely chopped raw mango
¼ cup sev
Salt, to taste

Method

1. **To make chaat masala 3**, combine the cumin and coriander seeds in a pan and roast for a few minutes over medium heat. Put the toasted spices into the jar of a mixer-grinder and put the pan back on the heat.
2. In the same pan, heat the oil before adding the boriya chillies. Roast for a few minutes, making sure the chillies don't darken. Add the roasted chillies to the mixer-grinder and blend into a fine powder. Add citric acid and salts and blend once again. Transfer this chaat masala into a bowl.
3. **To assemble**, cut the potatoes in half and butter the flat sides. Place a few tomato slices on one half of the potato before closing it with the other half.
4. Place the potato bombs on a plate. Top them with the three chutneys, onion, raw mango, and sev. Sprinkle with the prepared fiery chaat masala, add a little salt and serve.

CLASSIC CHAATS FROM INDIA 43

MAHARASHTRA

Chinese Bhel
Crispy noodles with tangy vegetables and sauces

Time taken: 20 minutes | Serves 4

Ingredients
1 tablespoon tomato ketchup
1 tablespoon red chilli sauce
1 teaspoon Schezwan sauce
1 teaspoon white vinegar
1 teaspoon dark soy sauce
1 tablespoon vegetable oil
1 tablespoon minced garlic
¼ cup sliced onion
¼ cup sliced carrot
¼ cup sliced cabbage
½ cup julienned red capsicum
½ cup julienned green capsicum
Salt, to taste
1 cup noodles of choice, boiled and deep fried

Method
1. In a bowl, combine the tomato ketchup with red chilli sauce. Vigorously whisk in the Schezwan sauce, vinegar, and dark soy sauce until you get a smooth dressing. Set aside.
2. Heat the oil in a heavy-bottomed pan over medium heat and sauté the minced garlic for a few minutes. Add the onions and sauté for another 3 to 4 minutes, until the onions turn translucent.
3. Add the carrot, cabbage, and red and green capsicum and stir fry for a few minutes making sure not to overcook the vegetables. They should retain their bite and colour.
4. Pour in the prepared dressing and toss well. Season to taste with salt and cook for another minute.
5. Add the deep fried noodles and toss through. Serve immediately as individual portions in shallow bowls.

CLASSIC CHAATS FROM INDIA 45

📍 MAHARASHTRA

Kolhapuri Bhadang Chaat

Puffed rice tossed with spices

Time taken: 25 minutes | Serves 4

Ingredients

3 cups puffed rice
¼ cup peanut oil
15 curry leaves
1 cup peanuts
5 tablespoons roughly chopped garlic
1 teaspoon turmeric powder
1 pinch asafoetida
2 teaspoons garam masala
2 teaspoons cumin powder
1 tablespoon coriander powder
2 tablespoons Kolhapuri chilli powder
¼ cup finely chopped onion
¼ cup finely chopped tomato
Juice of ½ lemon
Salt, to taste
2 tablespoons sev

Method

1. In a pan over low heat, dry roast the puffed rice until crisp, about 4 to 5 minutes. Transfer to a bowl.
2. Heat the peanut oil in a heavy-bottomed pan over medium heat and add the curry leaves. Flash fry for a few seconds. Using a slotted spoon, drain the leaves on kitchen towels before adding them to the puffed rice.
3. Toss the peanuts into the same oil and deep fry them until golden. Spoon the peanuts on top of the curry leaves.
4. Sauté the garlic in the same oil until crisp. Add to the bowl once golden.
5. Add a teaspoon of turmeric and a pinch of asafoetida to the same oil and stir. Cook for a minute before adding the garam masala and cumin, coriander, and Kolhapuri chilli powders. Stir and cook for a few minutes until fragrant.
6. Add the cooked spices to the serving bowl full of toasted goodness and toss. Use your fingers to help the flavour of the masala blend well through the dish.
7. Add the finely chopped onion and tomato, and a squeeze of lemon juice. Season to taste with salt. Mix well and garnish with sev. The chaat is ready to serve.

BIHAR

Bihari Chaat

Mashed potatoes and peas, amply spiced

Time taken: 25 minutes | Serves 2-3

Ingredients

FOR 3-SPICE CHAAT MASALA
2 tablespoons cumin seeds
1 tablespoon black peppercorns
4 dry red chillies

FOR THE CHAAT
1 tablespoon vegetable oil
2 teaspoons minced ginger
3 teaspoons minced garlic
1 teaspoon minced green chilli
2 teaspoons coriander powder
1 teaspoon turmeric powder
1 teaspoon red chilli powder
1 teaspoon roasted cumin powder
¼ cup finely chopped onion
¼ cup finely chopped tomato
Salt, to taste
1 cup boiled and mashed potato
1 cup boiled yellow peas
1 cup water
1 teaspoon dry mango powder
1 tablespoon 3-spice chaat masala (page 166)
1 tablespoon finely chopped coriander leaves

Method

1. **To make the chaat masala**, dry roast the cumin seeds, black peppercorns, and red chillies until fragrant. Let them cool and grind into a powder in a mixer-grinder. Keep aside.
2. Heat the oil in a deep pan over medium heat and add the minced ginger, garlic, and green chilli. Sauté for one minute and add the coriander, turmeric, red chilli and cumin powders. Sauté for another minute before adding the chopped onion and tomato.
3. Cook until the vegetables begin to soften, about 3 to 4 minutes. Season to taste with salt.
4. Mix the boiled potato and yellow peas into the masala and mash using the back of a spoon. Add up to 1 cup of water and dilute it into a thick paste.
5. Stir in the 3-spice chaat masala and dry mango powder and season once again. Continue to cook the mixture over medium heat for another 5 minutes.
6. Ladle into small bowls, finish with coriander leaves and serve hot.

BIHAR

Bihari Ghugni

Also called ghughri, a toss up of spiced peas and chutneys

Time taken: 40 minutes | Serves 2-3

Ingredients
1 cup sliced onion, divided
2 tablespoons chickpea flour
1 tablespoon vegetable oil
1 bay leaf
1 teaspoon cumin seeds
1 green chilli, finely chopped
1 tablespoon ginger–garlic paste
1 tablespoon coriander powder
1 teaspoon red chilli powder
1 teaspoon black pepper powder
1 teaspoon cumin powder
Salt, to taste
¼ cup water
1 cup boiled horse gram
2 tablespoons finely chopped coriander leaves
¼ cup freshly grated coconut

Method
1. Grind ¼ cup onion and chickpea flour in a mixer-grinder until it forms a paste. Set aside.
2. Heat the oil in a skillet over low-medium heat and add the bay leaf, cumin seeds, and green chilli. Cook until the seeds begin to crackle and add the rest of the onion and ginger–garlic paste. Sauté until the onions soften.
3. Stir in the coriander, red chilli, pepper, and cumin powders, followed by the onion–chickpea flour paste. Season well with salt.
4. Pour in the water, reduce the heat to low, and bring the gravy to a simmer. Add the boiled horse gram and cook for another 20 minutes.
5. Finish with fresh coriander and freshly grated coconut. Serve hot.

PUNJAB

Amritsari Bun Chaat

Burger bun sandwich with potato cakes and chutneys

Time taken: 25 minutes | Serves 2

Ingredients
2 burger buns, halved
½ cup butter, divided
2 potatoes, boiled and mashed
2 teaspoons red chilli powder
2 teaspoons coriander powder
2 teaspoons cumin powder
2 teaspoons chaat masala (page 166)
1 teaspoon black salt
Salt, to taste
1 onion, sliced
2 teaspoons red garlic chutney (page 170)
2 tablespoons date-tamarind chutney (page 168)
2 tablespoons mint-coriander chutney (page 168)
½ cup spicy peanuts
2 tablespoons pomegranate gems
½ cup nylon sev
½ cup finely chopped coriander leaves

Method
1. Butter both sides of the burger buns and toast gently on a skillet over medium heat. Set aside.
2. Mash the potatoes with red chilli, coriander and cumin powders, chaat masala and black salt. Season to taste with salt. Divide the mixture into 4 to 6 equal portions and shape each into a flat cake.
3. Return the skillet to medium-high heat and add the remaining butter.
4. Working in batches, pan fry the potato cakes on both sides until they are crunchy and golden brown. Place each cake on a toasted bun bottom and top with sliced onion. Drizzle the three chutneys over each.
5. Sprinkle the spicy peanuts, pomegranate gems, nylon sev, and fresh coriander over this and serve immediately with the bun top.

📍 RAJASTHAN

Rajasthani Mirchi Vada

Chilli fritters drizzled with yoghurt and chutneys

Time taken: 30 minutes | Serves 4

Ingredients

¼ cup yoghurt
½ tablespoon sugar

FOR THE VADA
1 cup mashed potatoes
1 green chilli, finely chopped
1 teaspoon chaat masala (page 166)
2 teaspoons fennel seeds
1 tablespoon coriander powder
2 teaspoons red chilli powder
2 teaspoons dry mango powder
1 teaspoon roasted cumin powder
Salt, to taste
10 large green chillies, slit open but not halved (Bhavnagari mirchi)
1 cup chickpea flour
Water to dilute
Sunflower or any neutral oil for frying
½ cup green chilli–coriander chutney (page 170)
½ cup tamarind–jaggery chutney (page 169)
¼ cup red garlic chutney (page 170)
1 tablespoon sev
1 tablespoon chaat masala (page 166)

Method

1. Whisk the yoghurt with powdered sugar until smooth. Set aside until needed.
2. **To make the vada filling**, mix the mashed potatoes with green chilli and add chaat masala, fennel seeds, and coriander, red chilli, dried mango, and cumin powders. Mix well and season to taste with salt.
3. Stuff each green chilli with a big spoonful of the filling.
4. Sift the chickpea flour with salt and gradually add water until you have a pancake-like batter.
5. Heat the oil in a kadhai over medium heat.
6. Working in batches, dip the stuffed chillis into the chickpea batter and carefully add them to the hot oil. Deep-fry until golden. Use a slotted spoon and drain on kitchen towels.
7. Cut each chilli into 3 small pieces and place them on a serving platter.
8. Drizzle the sweetened yoghurt over the chillies and finish with spoonful of green chilli–coriander chutney, tamarind–jaggery chutney, red garlic chutney, sev, and a dash of chaat masala.

CLASSIC CHAATS FROM INDIA 51

UTTAR PRADESH

Banarasi Tamatar Chaat

Sweet and tangy tomato chaat, topped with syrup and sev

Time taken: 40 minutes | Serves 2

Ingredients
1 tablespoon ghee
1 teaspoon cumin seeds
1 green chilli, finely chopped
1 teaspoon poppy seeds
2 tablespoons ground cashew nuts
2 tablespoons khoya
½ teaspoon turmeric powder
1 teaspoon coriander powder
3 teaspoons red chilli powder, divided
2 teaspoons cumin powder, divided
1 cup finely chopped tomato
½ teaspoon black salt
1 teaspoon garam masala
3 teaspoons chaat masala, divided (page 166)
1 potato, boiled and mashed
½ cup + 4 tablespoons water
Salt, to taste

FOR THE GARNISH
3 tablespoons sugar
½ cup finely chopped coriander leaves
1 tablespoon finely chopped onion
¼ cup sev

Method
1. Heat the ghee in a heavy-bottomed pan over medium heat and add the cumin seeds and green chilli. Allow the seeds to crackle for half a minute before adding poppy seeds and cashew nut powder. Mix well.
2. Stir the khoya into this base. Sauté for about 2 to 3 minutes over medium heat until it turns golden. Add the turmeric and coriander powders, half the chilli and cumin powders, and sauté for another minute before adding the finely chopped tomato and black salt. Continue stirring over medium heat for 4 to 5 minutes.
3. Once the tomatoes soften, add the garam masala and half the chaat masala and mix again. Add the potato mash and stir it into the base. You can thin the mixture with up to ½ cup of water if it is too dense. Cook over medium heat for 4 to 5 minutes. Finish with salt to taste and set aside to cool.
4. **To make the syrup**, combine the sugar and 4 tablespoons of water in a heavy-bottomed saucepan and set over medium heat. Do not stir.
5. Once the sugar starts to melt (in about 2 minutes), add the rest of the cumin powder, chaat masala, and red chilli powder. Stir quickly and let it gently bubble until the sugar dissolves.
6. **To plate the chaat**, give the tomato mixture a good mix and check seasoning. Spoon into a deep bowl and drizzle the sweet sugar syrup on it. Finish with coriander, finely chopped onion, and sev.

MADHYA PRADESH

Indore Namkeen Chaat

Mixed savouries tossed with a spicy potato mixture

Time taken: 10 minutes | Serves 2-3

Ingredients

1 cup Indore namkeen (or any medium-thick spicy sev of your choice; available at grocery stores)
½ cup finely chopped onion
½ cup finely chopped tomato
½ cup finely chopped cucumber
½ cup boiled and cubed potato
1 teaspoon red chilli powder
1 teaspoon chaat masala (page 166)
Juice of 1 lemon
Salt, to taste
¼ cup finely chopped coriander leaves
¼ cup pomegranate gems
2 tablespoons nylon sev

Method

1. In a large bowl, toss the Indore namkeen with chopped onion, tomato, cucumber, and potato.
2. Add a teaspoon of red chilli powder and chaat masala, followed by a squeeze of lemon juice. Toss well to combine. Season to taste with salt.
3. Garnish with fresh coriander, pomegranate gems, and nylon sev before serving.

MAHARASHTRA

Cheeseling Bhel

Cheese-flavoured diamonds are tossed with a bunch of toppings

Time taken: 40 minutes | Serves 2-3

Ingredients

2 cups cheeselings (available at grocery stores)
¼ cup finely chopped onion
¼ cup finely chopped tomato
¼ cup boiled and finely chopped potato
½ green chilli, finely chopped
2 tablespoons masala peanuts (available at grocery stores)
2 tablespoons spicy dal (available at grocery stores)
1 teaspoon chaat masala (page 166)
1 teaspoon red chilli powder
½ tablespoon lemon juice
1 tablespoon finely chopped coriander leaves
1 tablespoon finely chopped mint leaves
1 teaspoon sev

Method

1. In a shallow serving bowl, combine the cheeselings with finely chopped onion, tomato, and potato.
2. Spoon over the chopped green chilli, masala peanuts, spicy dal and toss well. Add the chaat masala, red chilli powder, and lemon juice and toss once more.
3. Finish with a sprinkle of coriander and mint leaves and garnish with sev before serving.

📍 MAHARASHTRA

Vitamin Bhel

Mixed sprouts, fruit and vegetables, topped with sev and spices

Time taken: 30 minutes | Serves 2

Ingredients

½ cup moong sprouts, soaked overnight and boiled
½ teaspoon turmeric powder
Salt, to taste
1 green chilli, finely chopped
¼ cup finely chopped apple
¼ cup finely chopped pineapple
¼ cup finely chopped cucumber
¼ cup finely chopped onion
¼ cup finely chopped tomato
1 teaspoon red chilli powder
1 teaspoon chaat masala (page 166)
1 cup toasted puffed rice
½ cup sev
¼ cup finely chopped coriander leaves
1 tablespoon finely chopped mint leaves
Juice of ½ lemon

Method

1. In a pan over medium heat, bring 1 cup of water to a boil with turmeric and salt. Add the sprouts and cook until soft. Drain and transfer into a bowl.
2. Once the sprouts have cooled slightly, add the chopped green chilli, apple, pineapple, cucumber, onion, and tomato and lightly toss to mix.
3. Sprinkle over the red chilli powder, chaat masala, and salt and toss again. Finish by adding puffed rice and sev and give it one final mix.
4. Garnish with coriander and mint leaves and a squeeze of lemon juice before serving.

CLASSIC CHAATS FROM INDIA 55

MAHARASHTRA

Healthy Moth Ki Chaat

Mixed sprouts topped with a tangy, spiced potato mixture

Time taken: 10 minutes | Serves 2

Ingredients

1 cup sprouted and boiled Turkish bean (moth/matki)
½ cup dal moth namkeen (available at grocery stores)
¼ cup finely chopped onion
¼ cup finely chopped potato
¼ cup finely chopped tomato
1 tablespoon finely chopped mint leaves
1 tablespoon finely chopped coriander leaves
1 teaspoon chaat masala (page 166)
½ tablespoon chaat masala 3 (page 167)
Juice of 1 lemon
Salt, to taste
1 tablespoon pomegranate gems
1 tablespoon sev

Method

1. In a wide bowl, combine the boiled matki with dal moth namkeen. Add the chopped onion, potato and tomato and toss lightly.
2. Top with mint and coriander leaves, chaat masala, and chaat masala 3.
3. Finish with a squeeze of lemon juice, a little salt, pomegranate gems, and generous sprinkles of sev.
4. Toss once more and serve.

📍 UTTAR PRADESH

Sweet Potato Tikki Chaat

Sweet potato cakes drizzled with yoghurt and chutneys

Time taken: 25 minutes | Serves 4

Ingredients
½ cup yoghurt
1 teaspoon sugar
3 boiled and mashed sweet potatoes
1 tablespoon chaat masala (page 166)
1 teaspoon roasted cumin powder
1 tablespoon coriander powder
1 teaspoon red chilli powder
1 teaspoon garam masala
Juice of ½ lemon
3 tablespoons finely chopped onion, fried until crisp (birista)
Salt, to taste
Sunflower or any neutral oil for frying

½ cup tamarind–jaggery chutney (page 169)
½ cup green chilli–coriander chutney (page 170)
1 tablespoon spicy sev
1 tablespoon finely chopped coriander leaves
1 tablespoon finely chopped mint leaves
2 tablespoons pomegranate gems
1 tablespoon chaat masala (page 166)
1 tablespoon alfalfa sprouts

Method
1. Whisk the yoghurt with a teaspoon of sugar until smooth. Set aside.
2. In a large bowl, combine the sweet potato with the chaat masala, cumin, coriander, and red chilli powders, garam masala, lemon juice, birista, and salt. Mash well.
3. Heat the oil in a pan over medium heat.
4. Roll the prepared mixture into palm-sized patties and shallow fry in hot oil. Drain using kitchen towels before transferring to a serving platter.
5. Top the tikkis with the sweetened yoghurt followed by drizzles of the chutneys and generous sprinkles of spicy sev and coriander leaves, mint leaves, and pomegranate gems.
6. Garnish with chaat masala and alfalfa sprouts and serve.

Tulsi-Cinnamon Fruit Chaat

Ayurveda-approved tangy spiced fruit salad

Time taken: 10 minutes | Serves 2

Ingredients
1 cup cubed apple
1 cup cubed pineapple
1 banana, sliced (optional)
3 tablespoons pomegranate gems
Juice of ½ lemon
1 pinch chaat masala (page 166)
1 teaspoon cinnamon powder
1 pinch black salt
1 tablespoon finely chopped Indian basil (tulsi)

Method
1. In a serving bowl, combine the apple, pineapple, banana (if using), and pomegranate gems.
2. Squeeze the lemon juice over the fruits and toss well.
3. Sprinkle over the chaat masala, cinnamon powder, and black salt; toss again.
4. Garnish with basil leaves and serve.

PAN-INDIA

Peanut Chaat

Boiled peanuts tossed with a spicy potato mixture

Time taken: 10 minutes | Serves 2

Ingredients
2 cups boiled peanuts
1 teaspoon red chilli powder
1 tablespoon chaat masala (page 166)
1 tablespoon cumin powder
Juice of 1 lemon
¼ cup boiled and chopped potato
¼ cup boiled and chopped tomato
2 tablespoons finely chopped onion
1 tablespoon masala peanuts (available at grocery stores)
Salt, to taste
1 tablespoon finely chopped coriander leaves
1 tablespoon finely chopped mint leaves
1 tablespoon pomegranate gems
1 tablespoon sev

Method
1. In a wide serving bowl, combine the boiled peanuts with red chilli powder, chaat masala, cumin powder, and lemon juice.
2. Add the chopped potatoes, tomatoes, onions, and masala peanuts; toss well. Season to taste with salt and toss again.
3. Finish with coriander leaves, mint leaves, pomegranate gems, and sev.

CLASSIC CHAATS FROM INDIA 59

📍 MAHARASHTRA

Kala Chana Chaat

Buttered black chickpeas tossed with a spicy potato mixture

Time taken: 20 minutes | Serves 2

Ingredients

1 teaspoon red chilli powder
1 teaspoon coriander powder
1 teaspoon roasted cumin powder
1 teaspoon kala chana chaat masala (page 167)
½ teaspoon black salt
2 tablespoons butter
½ tablespoon grated ginger
1 pinch asafoetida
1 cup boiled black chickpeas
½ cup boiled and cubed potato
¼ cup finely chopped tomato
¼ cup finely chopped onion
½ green chilli, finely chopped
Salt, to taste
¼ cup finely chopped coriander leaves
Juice of ½ lemon

Method

1. Stir the red chilli, coriander and roasted cumin powders, chaat masala, and black salt in a glass along with 3 tablespoons of water to create a spice syrup.
2. Heat the butter in a medium-sized skillet over gentle heat. Add the grated ginger and sauté for 1 minute. Add a pinch of asafoetida and stir.
3. Pour in the spice syrup and mix. Allow it to cook for 3 minutes over medium heat before adding the boiled black chickpeas. Toss well so the spices coat thoroughly. Remove from heat and stir in the cubed potatoes, chopped tomatoes, onions, and green chilli. Season to taste with salt.
4. Garnish with fresh coriander leaves and a squeeze of lemon juice, and serve.

◉ DELHI

Kulle Ki Chaat

Fruit and vegetable cups filled with hung curd and chutneys

Time taken: 20 minutes | Serves 2-3

Ingredients
1 cucumber, peeled and halved
1 pineapple, peeled
2 tomatoes, halved
1½ cup hung curd
2 teaspoons powdered sugar
1 teaspoon roasted cumin powder
1 teaspoon red chilli powder
¼ cup roughly chopped mint leaves
¼ cup puffed rice
½ cup tamarind–jaggery chutney (page 169)
½ cup green chilli–coriander chutney (page 170)
Salt, to taste
1 cup pomegranate gems
½ cup sprouts
¼ cup roasted and crushed peanuts
1 tablespoon butter
¼ cup sev
Juice of ½ lemon
1 tablespoon chaat masala (page 166)
1 tablespoon julienned ginger

Method
1. Cut the cucumber, pineapple and tomatoes into thick slices and core the centres to make buckets, making sure the bottoms of the slices are sealed. Place the fruit and vegetable baskets in cold water until needed.
2. Whisk the hung curd with sugar in a large bowl until smooth. Stir in cumin and red chilli powders, mint leaves, puffed rice and both the chutneys. Season to taste with salt. Add the pomegranate gems, sprouts, and roasted peanuts. Combine well.
3. Heat a tablespoon of butter on a grill pan over medium heat and gently grill the tomatoes, pineapple, and cucumber until grill marks appear. This may take about 3 to 4 minutes.
4. Place the grilled fruits and vegetables on a flat plate and top them with generous scoops of the curd filling. Garnish with sev, lemon juice, chaat masala and ginger, and serve.

BY CHEF SARANSH GOILA

UTTAR PRADESH

Tawa Paneer Chaat

Marinated cottage cheese topped with cream and spices

Time taken: 50 minutes | Serves 4

Ingredients

FOR THE TAWA PANEER
½ cup hung curd
1 tablespoon ginger–garlic paste
½ tablespoon red chilli powder
½ tablespoon coriander powder
1 teaspoon dry mango powder
1 teaspoon cumin powder
1 teaspoon garam masala
1 teaspoon dried fenugreek leaves
1 tablespoon tikka masala
Salt, to taste
½ cup cubed cottage cheese
½ cup cubed green capsicum
5 tablespoons butter

FOR THE CHAAT
1 tablespoon finely chopped coriander leaves
1 tablespoon finely chopped mint leaves
¼ cup finely sliced onion
1 tablespoon crumbled khoya
1 tablespoon cream
1 teaspoon chaat masala (page 166)
1 tablespoon pomegranate gems
1 onion, finely sliced and fried (birista)
1 tablespoon julienned ginger
Juice of ½ lemon

Method

1. Whisk the hung curd with ginger–garlic paste, red chilli, coriander, dry mango, and cumin powders, garam masala, dried fenugreek leaves, and tikka masala; season to taste with salt. Stir in the cottage cheese and capsicum and set aside for 30 minutes.
2. Heat the butter in a pan over medium heat and shallow fry the marinated capsicum and paneer in batches until the masala coating them is cooked. This should take about 4 to 5 minutes on each side.
3. Place the cooked capsicum and paneer in a shallow bowl and add coriander and mint leaves, followed by finely sliced onion, crumbled khoya, and cream. Stir thoroughly.
4. Garnish with chaat masala, pomegranate gems, birista, ginger, and lemon juice and serve.

CLASSIC CHAATS FROM INDIA 63

UTTAR PRADESH

Raj Kachori

Crispy fried pastry with a delightful yoghurt, chickpea, and potato stuffing

Time taken: 45 minutes | Serves 2-3

Ingredients

FOR THE KACHORI
1 cup refined flour
1 cup semolina
½ teaspoon baking powder
Sunflower or any neutral oil for frying
½ cup water
Salt, to taste

FOR THE STUFFING
1 cup yoghurt
2 tablespoons powdered sugar
1 teaspoon black salt
1 teaspoon red chilli powder
¼ cup boiled and cubed potato
¼ cup finely chopped tomato
¼ cup finely chopped onion
2 tablespoons sprouted moong
2 tablespoons ragda (page 71)
½ cup tamarind–jaggery chutney (page 169)
½ cup green chilli–coriander chutney (page 170)
1 tablespoon chaat masala (page 166)
1 teaspoon roasted cumin powder
1 teaspoon red chilli powder
¼ cup spicy chana dal (available at grocery stores)
¼ cup sev
1 tablespoon finely chopped coriander leaves
1 teaspoon boondi (available at grocery stores)
1 tablespoon pomegranate gems
1 teaspoon black salt

Method

1. Whisk the yoghurt with sugar, black salt, and red chilli powder until smooth. Set aside until needed.
2. Sift the refined flour with semolina and baking powder. Gently warm a teaspoon of oil and add to the flour. Knead it into a soft dough, slowly adding water. Cover the bowl and allow the dough to rest for 15 minutes. Meanwhile, heat the oil in a kadhai over medium heat.
3. Break sections of the dough and roll them into large puris, the size of your palm. Deep fry them until golden brown. With the help of a slotted spoon, pour oil on top of the puris, and allow them to puff up. Drain on kitchen towels. The puris will crisp as they cool down to room temperature.
4. Gently crack the top of the puris with your fingers and stuff them with boiled potatoes, tomato, onion, sprouts, and ragda. Place on a serving platter.
5. Drizzle the stuffed puris with spiced yoghurt, followed by the chutneys. Finish with sprinkles of chaat masala, roasted cumin and red chilli powders, followed by spicy chana dal, sev, fresh coriander leaves, boondi, pomegranate gems, and black salt.

CLASSIC CHAATS FROM INDIA 65

RAJASTHAN

Pyaaz Ki Kachori

Crispy fried pastry with onion and potato stuffing

Time taken: 1 hour 30 minutes | Serves 4

Ingredients

FOR THE KACHORI
1 teaspoon carom seeds
1 teaspoon fennel seeds
1 cup refined flour
3 tablespoons ghee
Lukewarm water to knead
Sunflower or any neutral oil for frying

FOR THE FILLING
1 tablespoon vegetable oil
3 teaspoons cumin seeds
1 teaspoon coriander seeds
2 teaspoons fennel seeds
1 green chilli, finely chopped
½ cup sliced onion
2 teaspoons coriander powder
2 teaspoons red chilli powder
1 teaspoon dry mango powder
1 teaspoon garam masala
1 teaspoon chaat masala (page 166)
½ tablespoon sugar
¼ cup boiled and mashed potato
Salt, to taste
1 tablespoon finely chopped coriander leaves

Method

1. In a large bowl, stir the carom and fennel seeds into flour. Add the ghee and rub through the flour with your fingertips until it resembles coarse sand. Slowly add water and knead into a tight dough. Cover the bowl with a damp muslin cloth and allow the dough to rest for 40 minutes.
2. Meanwhile, heat 1 tablespoon oil in a pan over medium heat. Add the cumin, coriander and fennel seeds, and green chilli. Allow the seeds to crackle before adding the onions. Sauté until they have slightly browned. This may take about 5 minutes. Add coriander, red chilli, and dry mango powders, garam masala, chaat masala, and sugar to the onions. Stir for another minute and tip in the potato mash. Mix well and season with salt. Keep aside.
3. Heat the oil in a kadhai over medium heat.
4. Divide the dough into equal parts and roll into balls. Flatten with your palm and roll the balls into thick rotis. Place a spoonful of the potato filling in the centre of each roti and pinch the edges together. Flatten once more and roll into a palm-sized kachori.
5. Deep fry the kachoris in batches until golden brown. Use a slotted spoon to remove and drain on kitchen towels.
6. Garnished with fresh coriander leaves serve with a chutney of your choice.

DELHI

Chole Chaat

Spiced chickpeas drizzled with yoghurt and chutneys

Time taken: 20 minutes | Serves 2

Ingredients

1 tablespoon butter
1 teaspoon finely chopped green chilli
2 teaspoons minced garlic
1 teaspoon minced ginger
1 teaspoon red chilli powder
1 teaspoon garam masala
2 teaspoons chole masala
1 teaspoon dry mango powder
1 cup boiled chickpeas
Salt, to taste
¼ cup finely chopped onion
1 tablespoon finely chopped mint leaves
½ tablespoon chaat masala (page 166)
Juice of 1 lemon
¼ cup whisked yoghurt
1 tablespoon green chilli–coriander chutney (page 170)
1 tablespoon tamarind–jaggery chutney (page 169)
1 tablespoon sev

Method

1. Heat the butter in a pan over medium heat and add the green chilli, ginger, and garlic.
2. Sauté for a few minutes before adding the red chilli powder, garam masala, and chole masala. Continue to cook for a few more minutes. Mix in the dry mango powder and boiled chickpeas, followed by a few tablespoons of water. Cook the chickpeas for another 5 minutes and season to taste with salt.
3. Spoon the chole into a wide serving bowl and top with finely chopped onions, mint leaves, some chaat masala, and a squeeze of lemon juice. Stir thoroughly.
4. Finish with drizzles of yoghurt, both chutneys, and a crown of sev.

UTTAR PRADESH

Tokri Chaat

Flour baskets filled with mixed vegetables, chutneys, and spices

Time taken: 40 minutes | Serves 2-3

Ingredients

FOR THE TOKRI
1 cup refined flour
1 tablespoon semolina
1 tablespoon oil
Lukewarm water to knead
Sunflower or any neutral oil for frying

FOR THE FILLING
1 cup boiled yellow peas
½ cup boiled and cubed potato
¼ cup finely chopped onion
¼ cup finely chopped tomato
¼ cup boiled sprouts
1 teaspoon chaat masala 3 (page 167)
1 teaspoon red chilli powder
1 teaspoon roasted cumin powder
Salt, to taste
¼ cup yoghurt
½ cup tamarind–jaggery chutney (page 169)
½ cup green chilli–coriander chutney (page 170)
3-4 tablespoons sev
¼ cup finely chopped coriander leaves

Method

1. In a wide bowl, combine the refined flour with semolina and a tablespoon of oil. Slowly add water and knead into a semi-tight dough.
2. Divide the dough into equal roundels and roll them into palm-sized rotis. Meanwhile, heat the oil in a deep pan over medium heat.
3. Stick each roti onto the outside of stainless-steel bowls or katoris with straight walls and carefully lower the bowls into the hot oil using tongs. Deep fry until golden brown. Allow them to cool once done, the fried dough will leave the bowls easily.
4. Place the fried bowls on a serving plate and spoon boiled yellow peas, potatoes, onions, tomato, and sprouts into each. Sprinkle them with chaat masala, red chilli powder, cumin powder, and salt. Pour enough yoghurt over each to cover the ingredients completely. Drizzle the chutneys on top and finish with sev and fresh coriander leaves.

CLASSIC CHAATS FROM INDIA 69

UTTAR PRADESH

Samosa Chaat

Samosas topped with spiced chickpeas and tangy chutneys

Time taken: 1 hour 40 minutes | Serves 4

Ingredients

FOR THE SAMOSA DOUGH
1 cup refined flour
1 tablespoon semolina
½ teaspoon salt
1 teaspoon carom seed, crushed
½ teaspoon fennel seeds, crushed
Cold water to knead
1 tablespoon ghee
Sunflower or any neutral oil for frying

FOR THE SAMOSA FILLING
1 tablespoon oil
2 teaspoons minced garlic
1 teaspoon minced green chilli
2 teaspoons roasted cumin powder
1 tablespoon coriander powder
1 teaspoon red chilli powder
1 teaspoon garam masala
1 cup boiled and coarsely mashed potato
¼ cup boiled green peas
Salt, to taste
1 teaspoon dry mango powder
2 tablespoons finely chopped coriander leaves

FOR THE CHAAT
1 cup ragda (page 71)
1 cup whisked yoghurt
¼ cup tamarind–jaggery chutney (page 169)
¼ cup green chilli–coriander chutney (page 170)
1 tablespoon chaat masala (page 166)
1 tablespoon finely chopped coriander leaves

Method

1. Sift the flour with semolina and salt in a large bowl; add carom and fennel seeds. Slowly add cold water and knead into a soft loose dough. Add a tablespoon of ghee and knead once more. Cover the bowl with a damp muslin cloth and allow the dough to rest for 40 minutes.
2. Heat 1 tablespoon oil in a pan over medium heat and add the minced ginger and green chilli. Sauté for a minute before adding the cumin, coriander, and red chilli powders. Add the garam masala and continue to sauté for another few minutes. Toss the mashed potatoes and peas through the spices and mash gently with a spoon. Season to taste with salt and finish with dry mango powder and fresh coriander leaves. Toss once more and set aside.
3. Break the dough into 4 to 5 small roundels and roll them into oblong rotis. Cut each roti in half so you end up with semi-circles. (You can also buy samosa dough sheets.) Heat the oil in a kadhai over medium heat for frying the samosas.
4. Roll each semi-circle into a cone, sealing the edges with a little water. Gently pinch the ends to secure the cone. Put a spoonful of the filling into the cone and seal it from the top by pinching the ends together. Deep fry the cones in batches until crisp; use a slotted spoon and drain on kitchen towels.
5. When you are ready, place a samosa or two on a serving plate. Gently press them with a spoon and pour a spoonful of ragda on top, drizzle with yoghurt, both chutneys, chaat masala, and fresh coriander leaves. Serve hot.

📍 MAHARASHTRA

Ragda Patties

Potato patties prepared mixture/ragda topped with masala chickpeas and tangy chutneys

Time taken: 40 minutes | Serves 4

Ingredients

FOR THE RAGDA
1 tablespoon sunflower or any neutral oil
1 teaspoon cumin seeds
½ green chilli, finely chopped
¼ cup sliced onions
1 tablespoon ginger–garlic paste
2 teaspoons red chilli powder
½ teaspoon turmeric powder
1 cup boiled white chickpeas
2 teaspoons garam masala
½ cup water
Salt, to taste
1 tablespoon finely chopped coriander leaves

FOR THE PATTIES
1 cup boiled and mashed potatoes
¼ cup flattened rice, soaked
1 tablespoon ginger–garlic paste
1 teaspoon dried fenugreek leaves
1 teaspoon pav bhaji masala
1 tablespoon finely chopped coriander leaves
1 tablespoon finely chopped mint leaves
½ green chilli, finely chopped
1 teaspoon roasted cumin powder
1 teaspoon dry mango powder
Salt, to taste
Sunflower or any neutral oil for frying

FOR THE TOPPING
¼ cup red garlic chutney (page 170)
¼ cup green chilli–garlic chutney (page 169)
¼ cup date–tamarind chutney (page 168)
¼ cup finely chopped onions
1 teaspoon chaat masala (page 166)
¼ cup nylon sev
2 tablespoons finely chopped coriander leaves
1 lemon, halved

Method

1. **To make the ragda.** Heat the oil in a deep pan over medium heat and add the cumin seeds. Allow them to crackle before adding green chilli, sliced onions, and ginger–garlic paste. Sauté for a minute and add the red chilli and turmeric powders. Continue to cook. Add the boiled chickpeas and garam masala and toss well. Add ½ cup of water to thin the mixture. Gently mash the ragda with a potato masher or fork to obtain a semi-coarse consistency. Season to taste with salt and garnish with coriander leaves. Keep aside.

2. **For the patties.** In a medium-size bowl, combine the potatoes with flattened rice, ginger–garlic paste, dried fenugreek leaves, pav bhaji masala, coriander leaves, mint leaves, green chilli, cumin and dry mango powders. Season to taste with salt.

3. Heat the oil in a heavy-bottomed pan over medium heat.

4. Scoop the potato mixture into medium-sized roundels and flatten them slightly with your fingers.

5. Shallow fry them in hot oil until crisp and drain on kitchen towels.

6. **To serve,** place the patties on a serving plate and top them with the ragda. Pour a generous spoonful of red garlic chutney over the ragda, followed by green chilli–garlic and date–tamarind chutneys. Add the chopped onions and finish with chaat masala, sev, and coriander leaves. Squeeze lemon juice over the chaat and serve hot.

GUJARAT

Fafda Chaat

Crunchy chickpea chips topped with vegetables, yoghurt and chutneys

Time taken: 15 minutes | Serves 2

Ingredients

FOR THE CHAAT
½ cup yoghurt
½ tablespoon powdered sugar
¼ cup finely sliced onion
¼ cup shredded carrot
Juice of ½ lemon
Salt, to taste
1 teaspoon chaat masala, more for garnish (page 166)
1 cup fafda (crunchy chickpea chips), broken into big pieces
¼ cup boiled and chopped potato
¼ cup green chilli–garlic chutney (page 169)
¼ cup date–tamarind chutney (page 168)
1 tablespoon sev
1 tablespoon finely chopped coriander leaves

FOR THE GREEN CHILLI TOPPING
2 tablespoons oil
1 teaspoon mustard seeds
1 pinch asafoetida
1 pinch turmeric powder
¼ cup slit large green chillies
1 teaspoon roughly powdered fenugreek seeds
Salt, to taste

Method

1. **To make the chaat**, whisk the yoghurt with sugar until smooth. Set aside.
2. Mix the finely sliced onion and shredded carrot in a bowl and add lemon juice, salt, and chaat masala. Toss well and set aside until needed.
3. **To make the green chilli topping**, heat the oil in a pan over medium heat and add the mustard seeds. Allow them to crackle and pop before adding asafoetida, turmeric powder, and chillies. Stir well and cook for a few minutes. Once the skin of the chilli begins to brown, add fenugreek powder and salt; continue to cook until the chillies are charred. Remove from heat and set aside.
4. **To serve**, break the fafda into large pieces and put them on a serving plate. Top with the spiced carrot and onion mixture, followed by the boiled potato. Drizzle the chaat with sweetened yoghurt along with generous dollops of both chutneys. Garnish with more chaat masala, sev, and coriander leaves.
5. Serve with charred chillies.

📍 UTTAR PRADESH

Palak Patta Chaat

Fried spinach leaves topped with yoghurt and chutneys

Time taken: 20 minutes | Serves 4

Ingredients

FOR THE PALAK PATTA
1 cup chickpea flour
1 tablespoon rice flour
¼ teaspoon carom seeds
¼ teaspoon turmeric powder
½ teaspoon red chilli powder, more to garnish
½ teaspoon chaat masala, more to garnish
Salt, to taste
Water to dilute
Sunflower or any neutral oil for frying
1 bunch of spinach, leaves trimmed

FOR THE CHAAT
¼ cup finely chopped onion
¼ cup finely chopped tomato
2 tablespoons yoghurt
¼ cup green chilli–garlic chutney (page 169)
¼ cup date–tamarind chutney (page 168)
1 teaspoon roasted cumin powder
1 teaspoon dry mango powder
1 tablespoon sev
Salt, to taste

Method

1. Sift the chickpea flour with rice flour, carom seeds, turmeric and red chilli powders, chaat masala, and salt. Slowly add water and whisk into a thin batter.
2. Heat the oil in a deep pan over medium heat.
3. Dip the spinach leaves in the prepared batter and deep fry, one at a time, until golden. This should take about 30 seconds. Use a slotted spoon and drain on kitchen towels.
4. **To assemble the chaat**, place the fried spinach leaves on a serving plate and top with onions and tomatoes. Drizzle yoghurt and both chutneys over the spinach leaves.
5. Finish with a sprinkle of cumin, dry mango and red chilli powders, chaat masala, salt, and a smattering of sev.
6. Serve hot and crispy.

RAJASTHAN AND GUJARAT

Kanji Vada

Lentil fritters soaked in fermented mustard water

Time taken: 45 minutes + 18 hours resting | Serves 4

Ingredients

FOR THE VADAS

1 cup split skinned green gram, soaked for 4 hours
3–4 tablespoons whole wheat flour (optional)
1 teaspoon roasted cumin seeds, crushed
1 teaspoon red chilli powder
1 teaspoon fennel seeds, crushed
2 teaspoons coriander seeds, crushed
1 tablespoon finely chopped coriander leaves
Salt, to taste
Sunflower or any neutral oil for frying

FOR THE KANJI

1 litre water
1 tablespoon split mustard seeds
2 teaspoons red chilli powder
2 teaspoons cumin powder
Salt, to taste

Method

1. **To make the vadas**, drain the soaked gram and pat dry with a kitchen towel. Use a mixer-grinder to grind the gram into a thick paste, adding a little wheat flour if the mixture is too thin. Do not use any water while grinding the paste. Whisk in cumin and red chilli powders, fennel and coriander seeds and leaves. Season to taste with salt and mix well.
2. Heat the oil in a kadhai over medium heat. Deep fry large ladles of the vada mixture in hot oil. Drain them on kitchen towels for a few minutes before resting in a bowl of water for 30 minutes.
3. **Make the kanji** by mixing split mustard seeds, red chilli and cumin powders and salt with water in a bowl. Stir well.
4. Drain the vadas from the water and press gently to release any water they may have absorbed. Tip them into the kanji and rest for at least 12 hours at room temperature.
5. Refrigerate for another 2 hours and enjoy the cold kanji vada.

CLASSIC CHAATS FROM INDIA 75

◉ DELHI

Ram Ladoo

Classic fried lentil balls and radish chutney chaat

Time taken: 30 minutes | Serves 4

Ingredients

FOR THE LADOO
½ cup split black gram, soaked overnight
1 cup split green gram, soaked overnight
¼ cup split pigeon peas, soaked overnight
1 tablespoon ginger-chilli paste
2 tablespoons radish leaves, blended to a paste
Salt, to taste
Sunflower or any neutral oil for frying

FOR THE RADISH CHUTNEY
½ cup radish leaves
½ cup coriander leaves
¼ cup mint leaves
1 teaspoon minced ginger
2 teaspoons green chilli paste
Salt, to taste
Lime wedges

Method

1. Drain the soaked lentils and place them in a mixer-grinder. Using as little water as possible, grind the lentils into a thick paste. Stir in the ginger-chilli and radish leaf pastes and season to taste with salt.
2. Heat the oil in a kadhai over medium heat.
3. Carefully drop spoonsful of the mixture into the hot oil and deep fry until golden brown. Use a slotted spoon and drain the ladoos on kitchen towels. Allow them to rest for a few minutes while you make the chutney.
4. **To make the chutney**, place the radish, coriander, and mint leaves in a blender along with the minced ginger and green chilli paste. Blend the ingredients into a smooth paste and season to taste with salt.
5. Serve the steaming hot ladoos with the radish chutney and wedges of lime.

BY CHEF PRATEEK SADHU

WEST BENGAL

Nimki Makha

Crushed diamond-shaped crackers topped with vegetables, yoghurt, and chutneys

Time taken: 1 hour 30 minutes | Serves 4

Ingredients

FOR THE BHAJA MASALA
1 tablespoon fennel seeds
1 tablespoon cumin seeds
2 teaspoons coriander seeds
1 green cardamom
1 teaspoon black peppercorns
1 clove
1 bay leaf

FOR THE NIMKI
1 cup refined flour
1 tablespoon semolina
1 pinch black pepper powder
Salt, to taste
½ teaspoon nigella seeds
½ teaspoon cumin seeds
1 tablespoon vegetable oil
Lukewarm water, to knead
Sunflower or any neutral oil for frying

FOR THE CHAAT
¼ cup boiled and cubed potato
¼ cup finely chopped onion
1 tablespoon finely chopped raw mango
½ cup tamarind–jaggery chutney (page 169)
½ cup green chilli–coriander chutney (page 170)
¼ cup yoghurt (optional)
Black salt, to taste

Method

1. **To make the bhaja masala**, in a pan over medium heat, dry roast the fennel, cumin, and coriander seeds along with green cardamom, peppercorns, clove, and a bay leaf. Allow the spices to cool and blend them into a fine powder. Keep aside.
2. Sift the flour with semolina, a pinch of pepper powder, and a little salt. Add the nigella and cumin seeds and a tablespoon of oil. Knead with water into a semi-soft dough. Place the dough in a bowl covered with a damp cloth and allow to rest for 30 minutes.
3. Heat the oil in a deep pan over medium heat while you roll out the nimkis.
4. Break the dough into balls and roll them into palm-sized circles, the size of a puri. Cut each puri criss-cross into three, shaping them like long diamonds.
5. Deep fry the nimkis until they are golden brown. Use a slotted spoon and drain on kitchen towels. Allow them to cool.
6. Crush the nimkis into a bowl and toss with potato, onion, and raw mango.
7. Spoon onto a serving plate and drizzle both chutneys over the mixture. Finish with yoghurt, a sprinkling of the prepared bhaja masala, and black salt. Serve.

MAHARASHTRA

Jacket Potato Chaat

Crispy potato shells stuffed with mixed vegetables

Time taken: 20 minutes | Serves 4

Ingredients

¼ cup yoghurt
½ tablespoon powdered sugar
Sunflower or any neutral oil for frying
4 large potatoes, halved
4 tablespoons butter

FOR THE CHAAT MIXTURE
¼ cup boiled and finely chopped potato
¼ cup finely chopped onion
¼ cup finely chopped tomato

FOR THE GARNISH
½ cup tamarind–jaggery chutney (page 169)
½ cup green chilli–coriander chutney (page 170)
¼ cup red garlic chutney (page 170)
1 tablespoon sev
¼ cup papdi, crushed (page 174)
2 tablespoons finely chopped coriander leaves
2 tablespoons finely sliced raw mango
2 tablespoons spicy dal namkeen (available at grocery stores)
1 tablespoon chaat masala (page 166)
Black salt, to taste

Method

1. Whisk the yoghurt with powdered sugar and keep aside.
2. Heat the oil in a heavy-bottomed saucepan over medium heat. Scoop the flesh out of the halved potatoes and deep fry the shells until they are golden brown. Pour a tablespoon of butter on the inside of each shell while hot.
3. Combine the finely chopped onion, potato, and tomato in a bowl and set aside.
4. Place the crispy potato shells on a serving plate and fill them with the prepared chaat mix. Cover each with the sweet yoghurt followed by drizzles of tamarind-jaggery, chilli–coriander, and red garlic chutneys.
5. Top with sev, papdi and coriander leaves and finish with raw mango, spicy dal namkeen, chaat masala, and black salt.

CLASSIC CHAATS FROM INDIA

GUJARAT

Kand Tikki Chaat

Yam cakes with sweetened yoghurt and chutneys

Time taken: 30 minutes | Serves 4

Ingredients

¼ cup yoghurt
½ tablespoon sugar
1 cup boiled and mashed purple yam
½ tablespoon ginger–garlic paste
1 teaspoon dry mango powder
1 teaspoon garam masala
2 teaspoons chaat masala, more for garnish
1 teaspoon red chilli powder
¼ cup finely sliced onions
1 tablespoon khoya
2 teaspoons finely chopped green chilli
1 tablespoon boiled green peas
Salt, to taste
Sunflower or any neutral oil for frying

FOR THE CHAAT
½ cup tamarind–jaggery chutney (page 169)
½ cup green chilli–coriander chutney (page 170)
¼ cup red garlic chutney (page 170)
1 tablespoon pomegranate gems
1 tablespoon sev
2 tablespoon finely chopped coriander leaves
1 teaspoon chaat masala (page 166)

Method

1. Whisk the yoghurt with powdered sugar and keep aside.
2. **To make the tikkis,** mix the mashed yam with the ginger–garlic paste, mango powder, garam masala, chaat masala, red chilli powder, sliced onion, khoya, green chilli, green peas, and season with salt.
3. Heat the oil in a heavy-bottomed pan over medium heat.
4. Take large spoonsful of the mixture and roll them into 4 to 5 tikkis. Shallow fry in hot oil on both sides until golden brown. This should take about 7 to 8 minutes. Drain using kitchen towels.
5. **To serve,** place the tikkis on a serving plate. Pour the sweetened yoghurt over the tikkis followed by drizzles of tamarind-jaggery, chilli–coriander, and red garlic chutneys.
6. Garnish with pomegranate gems, sev, coriander leaves, and chaat masala.

◉ UTTAR PRADESH

Karari Bhindi Chaat

Crispy okra drizzled with yoghurt and chutneys

Time taken: 20 minutes | Serves 4

Ingredients

FOR THE CRISPY OKRA
1½ cups okra
½ cup chickpea flour
3 tablespoons rice flour
3 teaspoons chaat masala, more for garnish
1 teaspoon roasted cumin powder
2 teaspoons red chilli powder
1 teaspoon fennel powder
1 teaspoon dry mango powder
1 teaspoon garam masala
Salt, to taste, more for garnish
2 teaspoons vegetable oil
Sunflower or any neutral oil for frying

FOR THE CHAAT
½ cup yoghurt
2 tablespoons mint–coriander chutney (page 168)
1 teaspoon date–tamarind chutney (page 168)
¼ cup finely chopped onion
¼ cup finely chopped tomato
1 tablespoon finely chopped coriander leaves
1 tablespoon sev
Juice of ½ lemon

Method

1. Cut the tops of the okra and slice each into four slender strips.
2. Sift the chickpea flour thoroughly with rice flour, chaat masala, cumin, red chilli, fennel, and dry mango powders, garam masala, and salt.
3. Coat the okra with 2 teaspoons of oil before tossing the strips through the flour mixture. The oil will help the mixture coat the vegetable well.
4. Heat the oil in a deep pan over medium heat.
5. Drop fry the okra in hot oil until crisp and golden brown. This should take about 2 to 3 minutes, be careful not to burn it or it will turn bitter. Drain on kitchen towels.
6. Scatter the crispy okra onto a serving plate and drizzle with yoghurt and the two chutneys. Garnish with finely chopped onion, tomato, coriander leaves, a sprinkle of chaat masala, sev, and a squeeze of lemon juice.

📍 PAN-INDIA

Pani Puri

Hollowed crispy balls filled with potato and tangy chutneys

Time taken: 2 hours | Serves 6

Ingredients

FOR THE PANI
2 cups mint leaves
1 cup coriander leaves
1-inch ginger, sliced
2-3 green chillies, finely sliced
¼ cup jaggery
1 cup ice cubes
1 teaspoon black salt
1 tablespoon roasted cumin powder
⅓ cup tamarind pulp
½ cup salted boondi (available at grocery stores)

FOR THE PURI
4 cups semolina
½ cup refined flour
Salt, to taste
Warm water to knead
Sunflower or any neutral oil for frying

FOR THE POTATO MIXTURE
1 potato, boiled and finely chopped
1 teaspoon roasted cumin powder
1 teaspoon red chilli powder
1 teaspoon black salt
1 teaspoon chaat masala (page 166)
½ cup sprouted and boiled moong beans

FOR SERVING
½ cup tamarind–jaggery chutney (page 169)
1 cup sev
1 cup ragda (page 71)

Method

1. **For the pani,** place mint and coriander leaves, ginger, green chilli, jaggery and ice cubes in a blender with a little salt. Blend into a smooth, thick paste, adding a few drops of water to loosen while grinding. Transfer the paste into a bowl and stir in black salt and cumin powder. Dilute the mixture with a few tablespoons of water and strain it. Strain the tamarind pulp into the pani, squeezing as much as you can out of the molasses. Add salted boondi and stir through. Transfer the pani into a jug and refrigerate until needed.

2. **To make the puris,** mix semolina with refined flour and salt, and knead it into a stiff dough using warm water. Cover the bowl with a damp cloth and allow the dough to rest for 30 minutes. Roll out the dough to 8 mm thickness and cut it into small circles with the help of a round cutter (approx. 3-inch diameter). It will yield 85 to 100 puris. Allow the dough to rest for a few more minutes while you heat some oil. Deep fry the puris until golden brown and drain using kitchen towels.

3. **For the potato masala mash,** combine the boiled potato with cumin powder, red chilli powder, black salt, and chaat masala. Mix with sprouted moong beans.

4. Serve the puri with chilled pani, tamarind–jaggery chutney, sev, and ragda.

BY CHEF RANVEER BRAR

CLASSIC CHAATS FROM INDIA 83

UTTAR PRADESH

Chicken Chaat

Marinated chicken tossed with spiced yoghurt mix

Time taken: 1 hour 30 minutes | Serves 4

Ingredients

FOR THE CHICKEN
½ cup thick yoghurt
1 tablespoon ginger–garlic paste
2 teaspoons red chilli powder
2 teaspoons roasted cumin powder
1 teaspoon dry mango powder
1 teaspoon chaat masala (page 166)
1 teaspoon black pepper powder
2 teaspoons tandoori masala
1 cup cubed boneless chicken
Salt, to taste
2 tablespoons butter

FOR THE CHAAT
1 tablespoon finely chopped onion
1 tablespoon finely chopped tomato
2 tablespoons crushed papdi (page 174)
1 tablespoon crushed spicy peanuts
1 tablespoon pomegranate gems
1 teaspoon sev
¼ cup yoghurt
½ cup tamarind–jaggery chutney (page 169)
½ cup green chilli–coriander chutney (page 170)
1 teaspoon chaat masala (page 166)
Juice of ½ lemon

Method

1. **To make the marinade,** combine the yoghurt, ginger–garlic paste, red chilli, cumin, and dry mango powders, chaat masala, pepper, and tandoori masala in a bowl. Add the chicken and season to taste with salt. Marinate it for 1 hour.
2. Heat the butter in a grill pan and cook the chicken over medium heat for 10 to 12 minutes.
3. Place the cooked chicken in a large bowl and add the finely chopped onion and tomato, papdi, peanuts, pomegranate gems, and sev. Toss well to combine before adding yoghurt and both chutneys. Toss once more.
4. Finish with a sprinkle of chaat masala, some pomegranate gems, and a squeeze of lemon juice. Serve in a wide shallow bowl.

CLASSIC CHAATS FROM INDIA 85

Crispy Lamb Bhel

Lamb tempura, masala potatoes and puffed rice with a burst of flavours

Time taken: 50 minutes | Serves 4-6

Ingredients

FOR THE LAMB TEMPURA
500 grams lamb rib rack
200 grams tempura flour
Sunflower or any neutral oil for frying
2 teaspoon chaat masala (page 166)

FOR THE BESAN CHUTNEY
4 tablespoons oil
2 green chillies, slit down the centre
½ teaspoon mustard seeds
1 teaspoon cumin seeds
½ cup sliced onion
2 tablespoons finely chopped ginger
1 ½ tablespoons turmeric powder
1 cup chickpea flour, whisked in 2 cups of water
Salt, to taste

FOR THE PALAK CHUTNEY
2 cups tightly packed spinach
½ cup chopped onion
1 cup coriander leaves
1-2 green chillies, chopped
1 tablespoon finely chopped ginger
2 tablespoons sunflower or any neutral oil
Juice of ½ lemon
3 cubes of ice
1 teaspoon dry mango powder
½ teaspoon cumin powder
Salt and sugar, to taste

FOR THE MASALA ALOO
1 tablespoon oil
2 tablespoons ginger–garlic paste
2 tablespoons green chilli paste
1 teaspoon red chilli powder
2 tablespoons chaat masala (page 166)
1 cup boiled and cubed potato
¼ cup chopped coriander leaves
Salt, to taste

FOR THE CHAAT
1 tablespoon puffed rice
2 tablespoons finely chopped onion
1 tablespoon finely chopped coriander leaves
1 tablespoon pomegranate gems
1 teaspoon chaat masala (page 166)
Juice of 1 lemon

Method

1. **To make the lamb tempura.** Slice the lamb ribs into large strips and dust them in tempura flour. Heat the oil in a deep pan over medium heat. Deep fry the lamb strips until crisp and golden brown. Drain using kitchen towels and dust with chaat masala.

2. **To make the besan chutney**, heat the oil in a pan over medium heat and add the green chillies and mustard seeds. Once the seeds begin to crackle, add cumin seeds, and allow them to sputter too. Add the onions and sauté until lightly golden, followed by finely chopped ginger. Cook for another minute and add turmeric powder. Whisk 1 cup of chickpea flour with 2 cups of water, and slowly add to the pan. Whisk until thickened, adding more water until the flour is cooked (3 to 4 minutes). Season to taste with salt. Pass through a strainer and set aside.

3. **To make the palak chutney,** blend the spinach, onion, coriander leaves, green chillies, ginger, oil, lemon juice, ice cubes, dry mango and cumin powders, salt, and sugar together in a blender. Strain and set aside.

4. **To make the masala aloo,** heat the oil in a heavy-bottomed pan. Sauté the ginger–garlic and green chilli pastes for 2 minutes before adding the red chilli powder, and chaat masala. Cook for another minute. Add the cubed potatoes and toss well in the masala, allowing the potatoes to coat evenly. Finish with fresh coriander leaves and a little salt.

5. **To serve**, place the lamb tempura on a platter and drizzle both chutneys followed by scoops of masala aloo. Finish with puffed rice, onion, coriander leaves, pomegranate gems, chaat masala, and lemon juice.

BY CHEF HUSSAIN SHAHZAD

CLASSIC CHAATS FROM INDIA 87

STREET FOODS OF INDIA

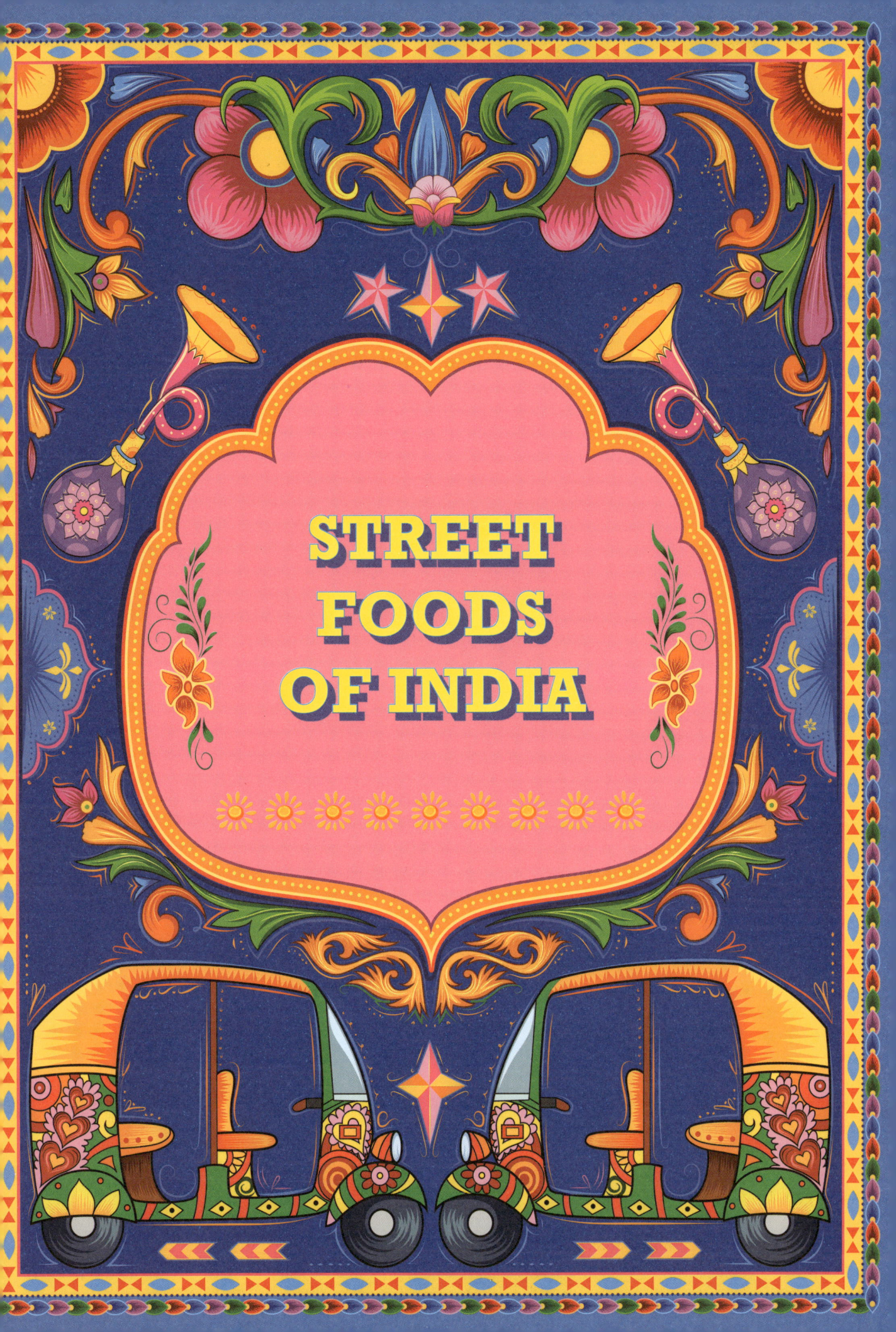

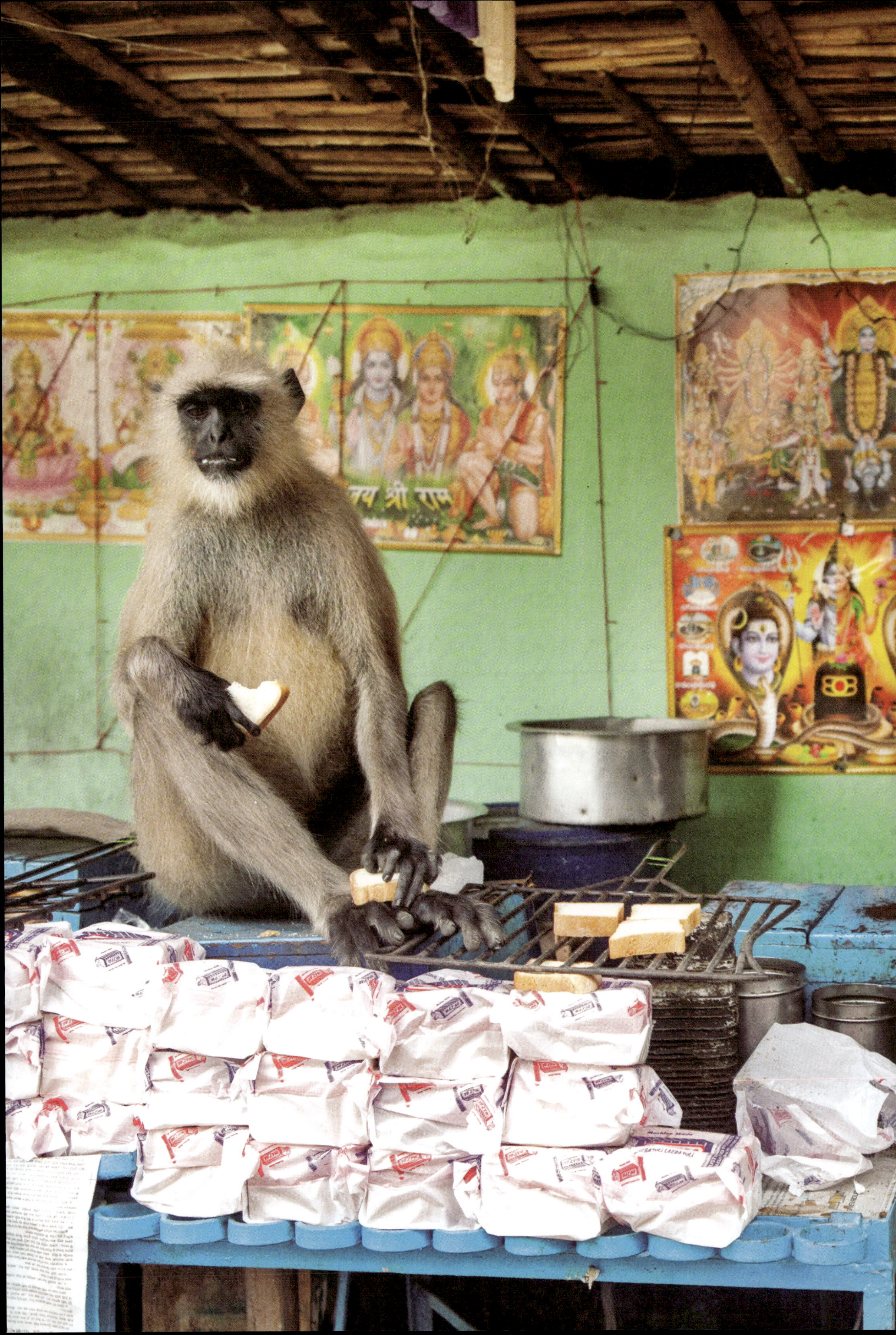

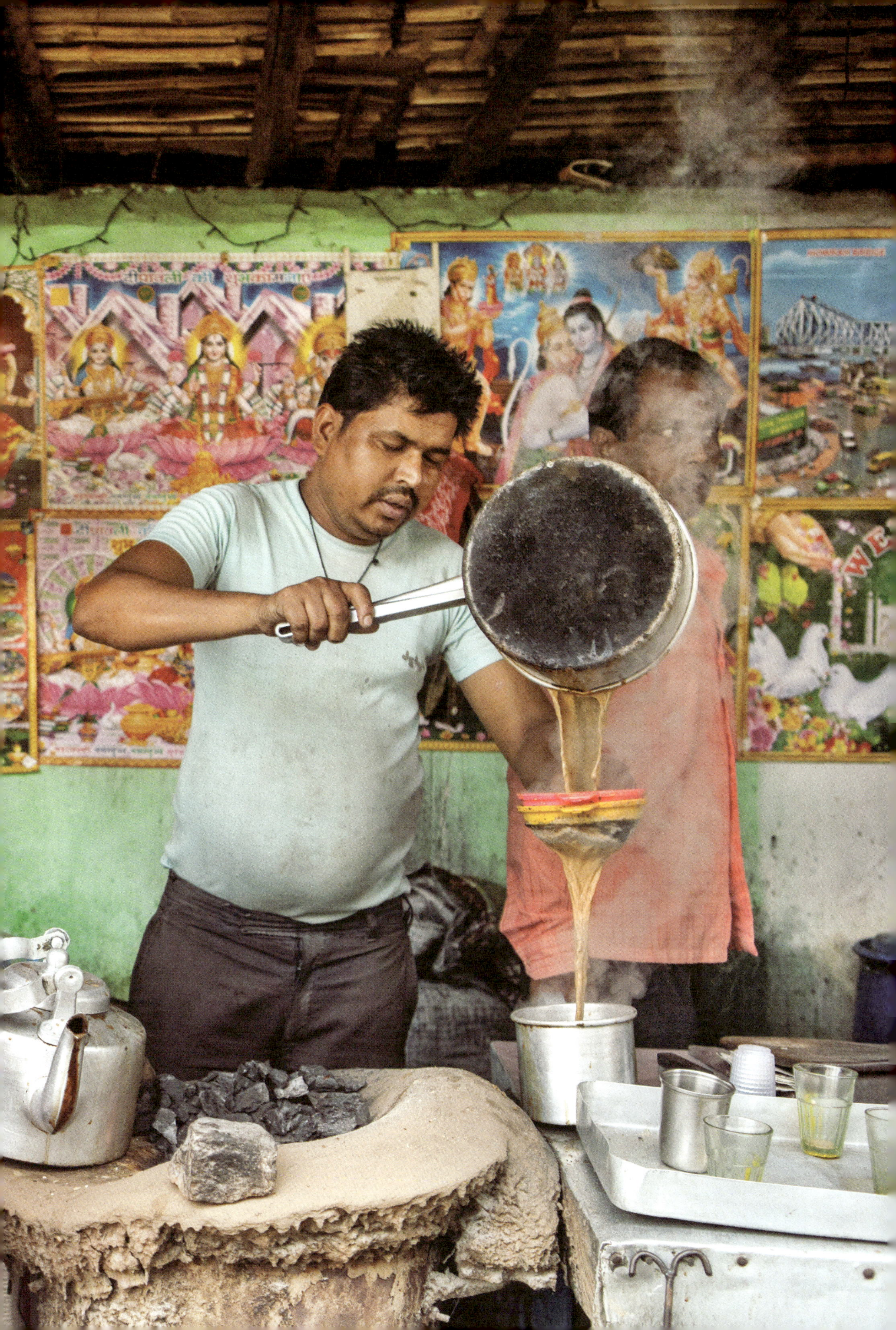

MAHARASHTRA

Sindhi Dal Pakwan

Flavoured puris served with dal, topped with tangy chutney

Time taken: 1 hour 10 minutes | Serves 2-3

Ingredients

FOR THE PAKWAN
1 cup refined flour
1 teaspoon crushed caraway seeds
2 tablespoons ghee
Salt, to taste
Lukewarm water to knead
Sunflower or any neutral oil for frying

FOR THE DAL
1 tablespoon vegetable oil
1 teaspoon cumin seeds
1 green chilli, finely chopped
5–6 curry leaves
1 pinch asafoetida
1 teaspoon turmeric powder
1 teaspoon red chilli powder
1 onion, finely chopped
1 tomato, finely chopped
2 cups boiled split pigeon peas
Salt, to taste

TO SERVE
½ cup green chilli–coriander chutney (page 170)
½ cup date–tamarind chutney (page 168)
½ cup finely chopped onion
1 teaspoon chaat masala (page 166)
¼ cup finely chopped coriander leaves

Method

1. **To make pakwan**, combine the refined flour in a bowl with a pinch of salt, caraway seeds and ghee. Rub the ghee through the flour mixture with your fingers until it resembles wet sand. Slowly add water and knead into a semi-soft dough. Cover the bowl with a damp muslin cloth and allow the dough to rest for 15 minutes.
2. Meanwhile, heat the oil in a kadhai over medium heat.
3. Break portions of the dough and roll them into palm-sized pakwans or puris. Deep fry the pakwans until golden brown and drain using kitchen towels. Keep aside at room temperature while you make the dal.
4. **To make dal**, heat one tablespoon oil in a saucepan over medium heat and add cumin seeds. Once the seeds begin to crackle, add the chopped green chilli, curry leaves and asafoetida, and cook for a minute. Sprinkle the turmeric and red chilli powders and mix well before adding the onion. Sauté until the onions turn golden, about 5 minutes.
5. Add the tomatoes and continue to cook for another 5 minutes before stirring in the boiled split pigeon peas. Cook the dal for another 10 minutes, adding water if it is too thick. Season to taste with salt and garnish with coriander leaves.
6. **To serve**, place each puri on a plate and top with the steaming dal and drizzles of green chilli–coriander and date–tamarind chutneys. Scatter finely chopped onions followed by a sprinkle of chaat masala and fresh coriander leaves.

STREET FOODS OF INDIA 93

MANIPUR

Manipuri Singju

Spicy vegetable salad garnished with fried savouries

Time taken: 2 hours 15 minutes | Serves 2

Ingredients

½ cup grated and soaked banana stem
or
½ cup finely sliced lotus root
½ cabbage, grated
¼ cup sliced onion
½ cup ragda (see page 71)
1 teaspoon powdered perilla seeds
1 tablespoon roasted chickpea flour
1 teaspoon red chilli powder
¼ cup mixed namkeen of choice
Salt, to taste

Method

1. Drain the banana stem and place in a muslin cloth. Create a tight potli (a small bundle), and squeeze as much water out of it as you can. Spread the banana stem on a tray and place it in the sun to dry for 2 hours.
2. Combine the banana stem or lotus root, whichever you are using, in a serving bowl along with grated cabbage and sliced onions. Toss a few times and set aside.
3. Coarsely pound the ragda with a potato masher or a pestle and add to the bowl. Toss to mix evenly.
4. Flavour the salad with powdered perilla seeds, roasted chickpea flour, red chilli powder, and the namkeen. Season to taste with salt and serve.

TAMIL NADU

Butter Sada Dosa

Thin crispy dosas generously topped with butter

Time taken: 20 minutes + 9 hours resting | Serves 4

Ingredients

FOR THE DOSA BATTER
½ cup split black gram
2 cups dosa rice
1 teaspoon fenugreek seeds
2 litres water
1 teaspoon sugar
1 tablespoon butter

Method

1. Combine the split black gram with dosa rice and fenugreek seeds and place in a large bowl. Cover entirely with water and soak for at least 3 hours before grinding into a smooth paste.
2. Allow the paste to ferment for 4 to 6 hours, or preferably overnight. Just before you are ready to cook, stir sugar into the batter.
3. Heat a griddle or a cast iron tava over medium heat. Take a teaspoon of butter and spread it on the pan. Pour a ladle of the dosa batter onto the pan and swirl to create a thin pancake. You can also use the back of the ladle to help spread the batter.
4. The dosa batter will release tiny air bubbles that pop as the dosa cooks. Spread another teaspoon of butter over the dosa once it is cooked, about 2 to 3 minutes and peel off the pan.
5. Serve piping hot with your favourite accompaniment.

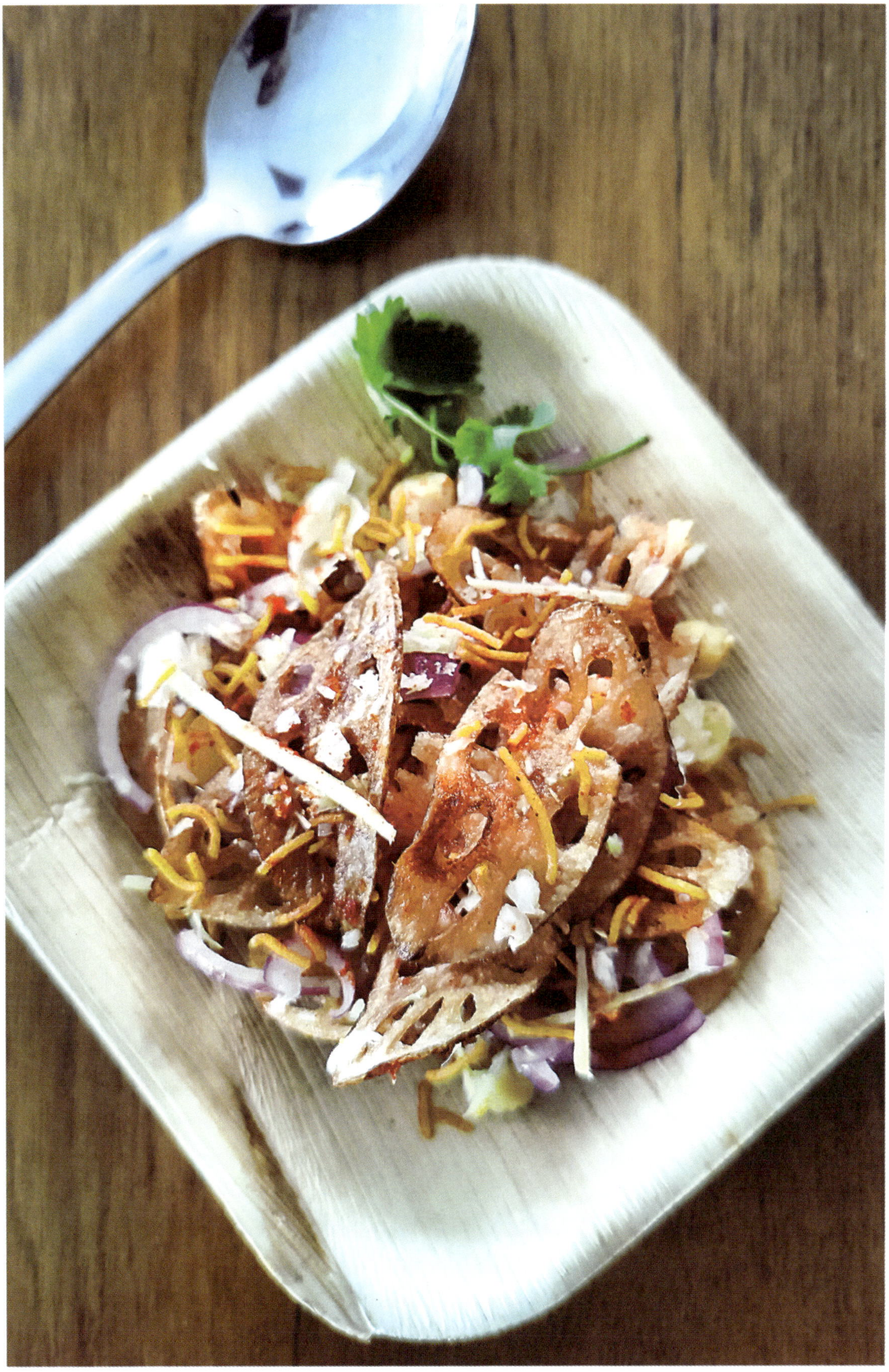

◉ MAHARASHTRA

Jinni Dosa

Crispy dosa bites stuffed with vegetables, cheese, and tangy sauces

Time taken: 30 minutes | Serves 2

Ingredients

FOR THE FILLING
1 tablespoon butter
1 cup dosa batter (page 94)
½ cup Schezwan sauce
1 tablespoon shredded cabbage
1 tablespoon grated carrot
1 tablespoon grated capsicum
2 tablespoons finely chopped onion
2 teaspoons finely chopped green chilli
½ cup finely chopped tomato
1 teaspoon tomato ketchup
1 teaspoon chaat masala (page 166)
1 teaspoon pizza spice mix
1 tablespoon finely chopped coriander leaves
1 tablespoon grated cheese

Method

1. Heat a griddle or a cast iron tava over medium heat. Take a teaspoon of butter and spread it on the pan. Pour a ladle of the dosa batter onto the pan and swirl to create a thin pancake. You can also use the back of the ladle to help spread the batter.
2. The batter will release tiny air bubbles that pop as the dosa cooks. Once the batter firms up, gently spread another teaspoon of butter over it, followed by the Schezwan sauce.
3. As the dosa cooks, strew it with shredded cabbage, carrot and capsicum, finely chopped onion, green chilli, and tomato. Drizzle tomato ketchup, and sprinkle with chaat masala, pizza spice mix, and fresh coriander leaves.
4. Sprinkle the grated cheese on top and allow to get crisp.
5. Peel the dosa off the pan and roll it into a tight cigar. Using a knife, cut the dosa into three pieces and serve hot with a chutney of your choice.

MAHARASHTRA

Kothambir Vadi

Squares of spicy dough and coriander mixture

Time taken: 25 minutes | Serves 4

Ingredients
5 tablespoons oil
2 cups finely chopped coriander leaves
1 cup chickpea flour
1 green chilli, finely chopped
2 tablespoons roasted and crushed peanuts
1 tablespoon white sesame seeds
2 teaspoons cumin powder
2 teaspoons coriander powder
1 teaspoon turmeric powder
½ cup water
Salt, to taste
1 tablespoon ginger–garlic paste
Sunflower or any neutral oil for frying

TO SERVE
½ cup tamarind–jaggery chutney (page 169)
Lime wedges
1 onion, finely sliced

Method
1. **To make the vadi,** toss the finely chopped coriander leaves in a bowl with the chickpea flour, chilli, crushed peanuts, sesame seeds, and cumin, coriander, and turmeric powders. Add water, a little salt and a tablespoon of ginger–garlic paste. Gently fold into a thick paste.
2. Prepare a steamer over medium heat. Pour the vadi mix into a rimmed plate and steam for 7 to 10 minutes. The vadi is done when a toothpick inserted into the batter comes out clean.
3. Heat the oil in a pan over medium heat. Cut the vadis into 1 inch squares and shallow fry them until golden on all sides. Drain using kitchen towels and place on a serving plate.
4. Serve with tamarind–jaggery chutney, wedges of lime, and finely sliced onion.

WEST BENGAL

Lal Aloo Wai Wai

Instant noodles served with potatoes and a fiery tomato gravy

Time taken: 50 minutes | Serves 2

Ingredients
2 cups water
5 tomatoes, roughly chopped
7 cloves of garlic, peeled
10–12 dry red chillies, divided
3 tablespoons mustard oil
1 tablespoon cumin seeds
1 tablespoon fennel seeds
2 tablespoons chickpea flour
2 cups diced and boiled potato
Salt, to taste
1 packet Wai Wai or any other instant noodles

Method
1. Heat the water in a saucepan over medium heat. Once the water reaches a simmer, tip in the tomatoes, garlic and all the dry chillies saving 2 for later. Simmer for 8 to 10 minutes, until the tomatoes soften. Cool the softened tomatoes in a blender and blend to a smooth paste.
2. Heat the mustard oil in a deep pan over medium heat and add the cumin and fennel seeds. Once they begin to crackle, add the remaining two dry red chillies. Sauté for another minute to temper the spices and add the freshly blended tomato paste. Continue to cook for another 8 to 10 minutes.
3. Meanwhile, mix the chickpea flour with just enough water to obtain a thick pancake-like batter. Pour the batter into the tomato mixture and stir. Allow the gravy to simmer for 7 to 8 minutes, adding water if it gets too thick, before tipping in the boiled potatoes and a little salt. Simmer for another few minutes and transfer to a serving bowl.
4. Heat a heavy-bottomed pan without any oil over medium heat. Crush the instant noodle packet with your hands before opening it. Shake out the crushed Wai Wai noodles as well as the dry spice mix that accompanies the noodles, along with any other seasoning or oil, into the pan. Lower the heat and toast the noodles and spices for a few minutes.
5. To serve, portion the toasted noodles equally into bowls and pour over the tomato gravy. Allow the noodles to soften for a few minutes and eat hot.

STREET FOODS OF INDIA 99

UTTAR PRADESH

Daulat Ki Chaat

An instant version of the traditional sweet winter treat from Delhi

Time taken: 20 minutes | Serves 2

Ingredients
2 cups cold milk (ideally refrigerated overnight)
1 cup full-fat cream
4-5 tablespoons sugar
2 teaspoons saffron strands
Pistachio and almond slivers for garnish

Method
1. Combine the cold milk, cream, and sugar in a deep bowl.
2. Whisk the milk with a hand blender stopping occasionally to gently remove the froth using a wide spoon. Place the froth in a bowl.
3. Repeat this process 7 to 8 times, continuously whisking and transferring the froth into the bowl.
4. Once the milk has halved, add the saffron and stir well. The milk will turn mild yellow.
5. Repeat the process of hand blending the sweet milk to make it froth. Transfer this yellow foam on top of the white milk foam and garnish with pistachio and almond slivers. Serve immediately.

MAHARASHTRA

Bun Maska

Fluffy bread buns slathered with ample butter

Time taken: 10 minutes | Serves 4

Ingredients
3 tablespoons salted butter
2 tablespoons heavy cream or homemade malai
1 teaspoon finely chopped raisins or tutti frutti
4 bread buns, sliced

Method
1. Combine the butter with the cream or malai in a bowl and mix until smooth.
2. Add the chopped raisins or tutti frutti to the butter and stir through. Spread a thick layer of the flavoured butter on the sliced buns and serve.

GUJARAT

Bohri Samosa

Filo pastry stuffed with minced mutton

Time taken: 1 hour 10 minutes | Serves 4

Ingredients

FOR THE SAMOSA
3 tablespoons vegetable oil
500 grams mutton mince
2 tablespoons ginger–garlic paste
1 teaspoon green chilli paste
½ teaspoon turmeric powder
2 teaspoons red chilli powder
1 piece coal
1 teaspoon ghee
¼ cup refined flour
2 tablespoons water
1 onion, finely chopped
½ cup finely chopped spring onions
1 tablespoon coriander powder
2 teaspoons roasted cumin powder
½ cup finely chopped mixed coriander and mint leaves
1 teaspoon chaat masala (page 166)
Juice of 1 lemon
Salt, to taste
Sunflower or any neutral oil for frying
10 sheets samosa patti (dough sheets)

FOR THE CHAAT
½ cup yoghurt
1 teaspoon green chilli–coriander chutney (page 170)
1 teaspoon chaat masala (page 166)
1 tablespoon pomegranate gems

Method

1. Heat the vegetable oil in a heavy-bottomed pan over medium heat. Tip the mutton mince into the pan and sear slightly before adding the ginger–garlic and green chilli pastes, and turmeric and red chilli powders. Sauté.
2. Cook the mince until all the water has evaporated and the meat is fully cooked. This should take about 20 minutes. Once it is cooked, transfer the mince into a bowl and cover it with a sheet of aluminium foil.
3. Heat a piece of coal on an open flame until it glows red. Carefully place the coal on top of the aluminium foil and pour a teaspoon of ghee over it. Cover the bowl (over the coal) and allow the minced meat to smoke for 30 minutes.
4. Make a slurry using ¼ cup refined flour and a little water.
5. Once the mince has been smoked, stir the finely chopped onion and spring onion greens through it. Add coriander and cumin powders, mint, and coriander leaves, chaat masala, and lemon juice and mix thoroughly. Add salt to taste.
6. Heat the oil in a kadhai over medium heat.
7. Spoon the mixture onto samosa pattis (or make fresh samosa cones, page 70) and fold them into neat triangles, sealing with a little slurry. Deep fry in hot oil until golden brown. Drain using kitchen towels.
8. Put the samosas on a serving plate and crack open from the centre. Drizzle the yoghurt and green chilli–coriander chutney over followed by sprinkles of chaat masala and pomegranate gems.

BY CHEF ALIAKBAR BALDIWALA

◉ MADHYA PRADESH

Indori Kees

Grated corn kernels tempered with coconut, cream, and spices

Time taken: 25 minutes | Serves 2

Ingredients
2 large corns, on the cob
2 tablespoons ghee
1 teaspoon cumin seeds
1 pinch asafoetida
1 green chilli, finely chopped
2 teaspoons ginger–garlic paste
1 cup milk
Salt, to taste
5 tablespoons freshly grated coconut
¼ cup finely chopped coriander leaves
½ cup pomegranate gems
5 tablespoons nylon sev

Method
1. Carefully grate the corn into a bowl using the medium side of a box grater. Set aside.
2. Heat the ghee in a skillet over low heat and add the cumin seeds and asafoetida. Once the seeds begin to crackle, add the green chilli and ginger–garlic paste. Sauté for 1 to 2 minutes.
3. Stir in the grated corn and slowly add the milk. Allow the mixture to boil until the milk has been completely absorbed. Season with salt.
4. Spoon into shallow bowls and garnish with freshly grated coconut, finely chopped coriander leaves, a scattering of pomegranate gems and nylon sev. Serve hot.

◉ PAN-INDIA

Cutting Chai

India's favourite drink made of milk, black tea, and cardamom

Time taken: 15 minutes | Serves 3-4

Ingredients
2 cups water
Sugar, to taste (optional)
2 teaspoons cardamom powder
1 teaspoon minced ginger
1½ teaspoons Assam tea leaves
½ cup milk

Method
1. Place a pan of water over medium heat and bring it to a gentle simmer. If you are using sugar, stir it into the water before adding the cardamom powder and minced ginger. Boil for 1 minute.
2. Add the tea leaves and continue to brew for another 3 to 4 minutes. Pour in the milk and simmer until the tea boils.
3. Strain the tea and serve it piping hot.

STREET FOODS OF INDIA 103

PUNJAB

Mango Lassi

Cold yoghurt-based drink flavoured with ripe mangoes

Time taken: 10 minutes | Serves 2

Ingredients
1 cup plus 3 tablespoons diced fresh ripe mango
1 cup yoghurt
½ cup cold milk
5 to 6 ice cubes
2 tablespoons powdered sugar (optional)
2 pinches cardamom powder (optional)
3 to 4 strands of saffron
2 teaspoons slivered pistachio

Method
1. **To make the lassi**, combine 1 cup diced mango with yoghurt and milk in the jar of a blender. Add ice cubes and blend until you get a thick smoothie-like consistency. Taste the lassi for sweetness and add a few spoons of powdered sugar if needed; the mango pulp is usually sweet enough.
2. Stir in the rest of the diced mango and pour the lassi into two glasses.
3. Garnish with a dusting of cardamom powder, strands of saffron, and/or slivered pistachio. Serve chilled.

KASHMIR

Kashmiri Kahwa

Hot dried fruit and saffron tea from the Himalayas

Time taken: 20 minutes | Serves 3-4

Ingredients
2 cups water
1 small cinnamon stick
4 green cardamoms
2 cloves
1 teaspoon dried rose petals
1 teaspoon Kashmiri green tea leaves
10 strands saffron
1 teaspoon finely sliced almonds or walnuts
1 tablespoon sugar (optional)

Method
1. Place a pan of water over medium heat and allow it to come to a rolling boil. Gently spoon in the cinnamon stick, cardamom and cloves, and continue to boil for 3 to 4 minutes.
2. Add the rose petals and Kashmiri tea leaves and steep for another 2 minutes before removing it from the heat.
3. Strain the tea into cups and sprinkle with saffron, slivered almonds or walnuts, and sugar if using. Serve hot.

📍 NORTH INDIA

Shikanji

Fizzy, chaat masala spiced drink

Time taken: 10 minutes | Serves 1

Ingredients
Juice of 1 lemon
2 tablespoons sugar
5 mint leaves, finely chopped
2 teaspoons shikanji masala (available at grocery stores)
4 ice cubes
1 glass club soda

Method
1. Pour the lemon juice into a chilled glass and add 2 tablespoons of sugar and the finely chopped mint leaves. Mix them together before adding the shikanji masala. Stir well.
2. Add a few ice cubes and pour the club soda over the mixture. Serve cold.

📍 PAN-INDIA

Aam Panna

Raw mango pulp sets the base for this cooling drink

Time taken: 10 minutes | Serves 3-4

Ingredients
2 green mangoes, boiled whole
1 cup crumbled jaggery
2 teaspoons cumin powder
2 teaspoons red chilli powder
2 teaspoons chaat masala (page 166)
6 mint leaves
1 liter chilled water
2 teaspoons black salt

Method
1. Peel the mangoes and scoop the flesh into a bowl. Mash it thoroughly before adding the crumbled jaggery, cumin and red chilli powders, and chaat masala. Stir well and continue mashing until the mixture turns into a pulp.
2. Spoon 3 tablespoons of the mango pulp into a tall glass and top with mint leaves. Pour in cold water and add black salt. Stir to make a refreshing, chilled drink.

📍 TAMIL NADU

Jil Jil Jigarthanda

An Indian summer drink made of milk and ice cream

Time taken: 10 minutes | Serves 2

Ingredients
¼ cup condensed milk
1 cup milk
3 teaspoons nannari syrup (available at grocery stores)
1 tablespoon khoya
2 teaspoons almond gum, soaked overnight
2 scoops vanilla ice cream

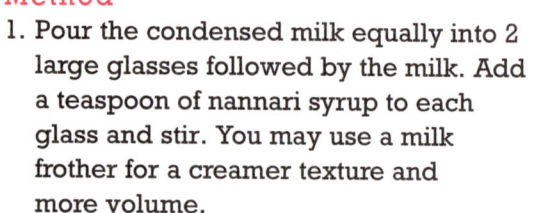

Method
1. Pour the condensed milk equally into 2 large glasses followed by the milk. Add a teaspoon of nannari syrup to each glass and stir. You may use a milk frother for a creamer texture and more volume.
2. Spoon in the khoya and almond gum. Top with a scoop of vanilla ice cream and half a teaspoon of nannari syrup.

📍 LADAKH

Thukpa

Tibetan noodle soup with mixed vegetables

Time taken: 30 minutes | Serves 2

Ingredients
3 tablespoons sunflower or any neutral oil
½ cup julienned carrot and French beans
1 onion, finely chopped
½ cup finely chopped spring onion
4 cloves garlic, minced
1 teaspoon minced ginger
1 green chilli, finely chopped
2 cups vegetable broth
1 teaspoon soy sauce
1 teaspoon honey (optional)
½ cup instant or hakka noodles
Juice of 1 lemon
Salt and ground black pepper, to taste

Method
1. Heat the oil in a saucepan over low heat and tip in the carrot and French beans. Sauté for a few minutes. Add the finely chopped onion and spring onion, minced garlic and ginger, and green chilli; continue to cook, stirring often, for another 5 minutes.
2. Pour in the vegetable broth, soy sauce, and honey. Stir well to combine.
3. Add the noodles and let the stock come to a boil before reducing the heat even further. Cover the saucepan and simmer the broth for about 15 minutes.
4. Ladle into wide bowls and season with lemon juice, salt, and black pepper. Serve hot.

STREET FOODS OF INDIA 107

MUMBAI

Frankie

Indian-style wrap with mixed stuffing

Time taken: 1 hour 10 minutes | Serves 4

Ingredients

FOR THE FRANKIE MASALA
1 tablespoon red chilli powder
1 teaspoon black pepper powder
1 tablespoon cumin powder
1 teaspoon carom seed powder
2 teaspoons coriander powder
1 tablespoon dry mango powder
1 teaspoon garam masala
1 teaspoon black salt

FOR THE ROTI
1 cup refined flour
Salt, to taste
1 teaspoon crushed carom seeds
1 tablespoon yoghurt
1 tablespoon oil
Water, as needed

FOR THE FILLING
5 tablespoons butter
1 teaspoon cumin seeds
1 green chilli, finely chopped
1 pinch asafoetida
2 teaspoons garlic paste
1 teaspoon red chilli powder
1 teaspoon chaat masala (page 166)
1 teaspoon tamarind paste
1 cup boiled and mashed potato
2 tablespoons tomato ketchup
1 tablespoon chilli sauce
1 teaspoon sugar
Juice of ½ lemon
¼ cup finely chopped coriander leaves
Salt, to taste

TO GARNISH
½ cup green chilli–coriander chutney (page 170)
½ cup finely sliced onion
¼ cup grated cheese

Method

1. **To make the Frankie masala**, stir the red chilli, black pepper, cumin, carom seed, and coriander powder together in a bowl. Add the dry mango powder, garam masala, and a teaspoon of black salt and combine. Set aside.
2. **To make the roti dough**, sift the refined flour with salt and add carom seeds and yoghurt. Knead into a loose dough. Sprinkle a tablespoon of oil over the dough and knead until it comes together. Cover the bowl with a damp muslin cloth and rest the dough for 40 minutes.
3. Meanwhile, heat a tablespoon of butter over medium heat and add the cumin seeds, finely chopped green chilli, and a pinch of asafoetida. As soon as the seeds begin to crackle, tip in the garlic paste and sauté for 1 minute. Add the red chilli powder, chaat masala and tamarind paste, and cook for another 2 minutes. Add the potato mash, tomato ketchup, chilli sauce, and sugar. Stir in lemon juice and 2 teaspoons of Frankie masala. Season to taste with salt.
4. Heat the remaining 4 tablespoons butter in a pan over medium heat. Roll 2 to 3 large spoonsful of the filling into oblong patties and shallow fry until the patties have browned on all sides. This should take about 5 minutes. Drain using kitchen towels.
5. Shape pieces of the dough into balls and roll them into large rotis. Heat a griddle over high heat and half cook the rotis.
6. **To assemble the Frankie**, spread the green chilli–coriander chutney on one side of each roti followed by a generous sprinkle of the Frankie masala. Place one or two patties (as desired) over the chutney, followed by finely sliced onion and grated cheese. Roll the roti into a Frankie and finish it by cooking once more on a hot griddle over medium heat for 2 to 3 minutes on both sides.
7. Serve hot.

TAMIL NADU

Thair Vadais

Dahi vadas from the South of India

Time taken: 45 minutes | Serves 4

Ingredients

FOR THE VADAI
2 cups split black gram, soaked in water overnight, drained
Salt, to taste
½ cup finely chopped curry leaves
2 green chillies, finely chopped
1 tablespoon peeled, crushed fresh ginger
1 tablespoon freshly squeezed lemon juice
½ teaspoon ground asafoetida stirred into ½ cup water

FOR THE SPICE MIX
2 dried red chillies
1 teaspoon cumin seeds
½ teaspoon black mustard seeds

FOR THE YOGHURT
2 teaspoons vegetable oil
½ cup finely chopped curry leaves
4 green chillies, slit
3 cups whisked yoghurt
1 cup water
Salt, to taste

Sunflower or any neutral oil for deep-frying

Method

1. **To make the vadai** batter, grind the split black gram into a paste in a mixer-grinder. Add the curry leaves, green chillies, ginger, lemon juice, asafoetida water, and salt to taste. Blend into a thick batter and set aside.
2. **To make the spice mix**, coarsely crush the dried red chillies, and cumin and mustard seeds in a mixer-grinder or a mortar and pestle.
3. **To make the yoghurt**, heat the oil in a kadhai over low-medium heat. Add the coarsely crushed spice mix, curry leaves, and green chillies. Cook for a few seconds.
4. Stir in the yoghurt, followed by water. Season to taste with salt. Transfer to a bowl and set aside.
5. **To finish the vadai**, clean the kadhai and heat the oil over high heat. Keep a bowl of cold water handy.
6. Gently lower spoonful of the batter into the oil and deep-fry the vadais until golden. Use a slotted spoon and drain on kitchen towels. Transfer the vadais to the bowl of cold water for just a few seconds. Remove and gently squeeze out the excess water. Repeat with the remaining batter.
7. Add the vadais to the spiced yoghurt and serve cold.

PUNJAB

Amritsari Kulfa

Dessert with ice-cream, vermicelli, and milk sweets

Time taken: 30 minutes + 4 hours resting | Serves 4

Ingredients

FOR THE KULFI
1 litre full-fat milk
¼ cup sugar
¼ cup condensed milk
2 tablespoons khoya
1 teaspoon cardamom powder
⅓ cup finely sliced almonds and pistachio

FOR THE KULFA
¼ cup rabdi
¼ cup firni
2 tablespoons Rooh Afza or rose syrup
¼ cup falooda sev (store bought and cooked as per instructions on the package)
1 tablespoon finely chopped assorted dried fruits
1 sheet edible silver foil

Method

1. Set 1 litre of milk mixed with ¼ cup of sugar to boil in a heavy-bottomed saucepan over low heat. Stir to make sure the sugar has dissolved completely and boil for 4 to 6 minutes before adding the condensed milk, khoya, cardamom powder, and sliced almonds and pistachio. Stir well. Simmer the milk over low heat until it has reduced by half and changed to a light beige colour (about 25 minutes). Turn off the heat and set aside to cool.
2. Once the milk has cooled, pour it into kulfi moulds and freeze until set. (Use small paper cups or any disposable cups if you do not have kulfi moulds.)
3. **To serve,** unmould each kulfi into a serving plate and top it with spoonful of rabdi and firni, a trickle of Rooh Afza, sprinkles of falooda sev, and dried fruits. Carefully place the silver foil over the top.

STREET FOODS OF INDIA 111

KASHMIR

Kashmiri Masalah Tchot

Kashmiri wrap filled with peas and spicy chutneys

Time taken: 45 minutes | Serves 2-3

Ingredients

1 cup dried white peas, soaked overnight
1 teaspoon turmeric powder
2-3 cloves
1 cup grated radish
1 onion, grated
2 teaspoons Kashmiri red chilli powder
1 green chilli, finely chopped
2 tablespoons finely chopped coriander leaves, divided
2 teaspoons dried mint leaves, divided
½ cup yoghurt
1 tablespoon walnut powder
2 to 3 lavasa bread (Kashmiri roti)
Salt, to taste
Water as needed

Method

1. Drain the soaked white peas and add to a pressure cooker along with a teaspoon of turmeric powder, cloves, and a pinch of salt. Pour in enough water to cover the peas and cook for 3 to 4 whistles over medium heat. Let the pressure release. Drain the peas and mash them gently. Set aside.
2. Combine the grated radish and onion to form a paste. Add a teaspoon of salt and set aside for 20 minutes. Divide and place in two separate bowls.
3. In the first bowl, add the red chilli powder, finely chopped green chilli, half the coriander leaves and dried mint to the paste. Combine and add salt and a spoonful of yoghurt. Mix well and set aside. The chutney will be red.
4. In the second bowl, mix the dried mint and coriander leaves to the onion-radish mixture. Add the yoghurt, walnut powder, and more finely chopped green chilli. Season to taste with salt and combine well. This chutney will be white.
5. **To serve,** spread the mashed peas generously on the lavasa. Add dollops of both chutneys. Roll, cut and serve.

STREET FOODS OF INDIA   113

MAHARASHTRA

Khopra Pattice

Potato patties stuffed with a coconut filling

Time taken: 25 minutes | Serves 2-3

Ingredients

2 cups boiled and mashed potato
3 tablespoons corn flour
Salt, to taste
½ cup freshly grated coconut
1 tablespoon desiccated coconut
¼ cup finely chopped coriander leaves
1 tablespoon finely chopped green raisins
1 tablespoon crushed peanuts
1 tablespoon finely chopped cashew nuts
2 teaspoons chilli–ginger paste
1 teaspoon sugar
1 teaspoon red chilli powder
1 teaspoon dry mango powder
Sunflower or any neutral oil for frying

Method

1. Combine the mashed potato with corn flour. Season to taste with salt.
2. In another bowl, toss the grated coconut with desiccated coconut, coriander leaves, green raisins, peanuts, cashew nuts, chilli–ginger paste, sugar, and red chilli and dry mango powders.
3. Divide the potato mixture into 8 to 10 soft rounds, flattening them with your hands into palm-sized patties. Press into each patty with your thumb, creating a small indent.
4. Spoon the coconut mixture into each patty, using the indent as a marker for the centre. Gather the sides of the patty and gently roll into a ball.
5. Heat the oil in a deep pan over medium heat. Deep fry the patties in hot oil until golden brown and drain on kitchen towels.
6. Serve hot with green chilli–coriander chutney (page 170).

SIKKIM

Sel Roti

Sweet, ring-shaped rice-flour fritters

Time taken: 30 minutes + 2 hours resting | Serves 2-3

Ingredients

2 cups rice, soaked overnight
½ cup ghee
½ cup powdered sugar
1 teaspoon cardamom powder (optional)
Oil for frying

Method

1. Drain the soaked rice and blend in a mixer-grinder into a smooth paste. Add the ghee, sugar, and cardamom powder (if using) and combine well. Cover the bowl and rest for two hours, checking on the batter once. Add 1 to 2 tablespoons of plain rice flour to the batter if it is too thin. Transfer it to a piping bag or squeezy bottle.
2. Heat the oil in a deep pan over medium heat. Pipe a large circle of the batter directly into the hot oil and fry until golden brown. Drain the rotis on kitchen towels.
3. **To serve,** place on a serving plate and sprinkle powdered sugar over each. Serve at room temperature.

MAHARASHTRA

Bombay Pav Bhaji

A mixed spiced vegetables mash served with buttered bun

Time taken: 40 minutes | Serves 4

Ingredients

FOR THE BHAJI
6 tablespoons butter, divided
½ cup finely chopped onion, divided
1 green chilli, finely chopped
1½ tablespoons minced garlic
1½ tablespoons pav bhaji masala
1 teaspoon garam masala
2 teaspoons red chilli powder
2 teaspoons coriander powder
½ teaspoon turmeric powder
¾ cup roughly chopped tomato
1 tablespoon red garlic chutney (page 170)
½ cup green peas, boiled
½ cup finely chopped capsicum
¼ cup cauliflower, cut into florets and boiled (optional)
1 cup boiled and mashed potato
¾ tablespoon
1 cup water
Salt, to taste
Juice of 1 lemon
5 tablespoons finely chopped coriander leaves

TO SERVE
3 to 4 pav, sliced
Lime wedges

Method

1. **To make the bhaji**, heat 2 tablespoons butter in a pan over medium heat. Add ¼ cup onion and green chilli and sauté for a minute. Add the minced garlic and cook for about 5 to 6 minutes until the onions have browned slightly. Add the pav bhaji masala, garam masala, red chilli, coriander, and turmeric powders, stirring well.
2. Lower the heat and tip in the chopped tomato, red garlic chutney, and a little salt. Cook until the tomatoes have softened, another 4 to 5 minutes before adding the peas, capsicum, and cauliflower (if using). Continue cooking.
3. Once the vegetables have softened, add the potato and mash well, using a potato masher, until you have a fine pulp. Stir in the dried fenugreek leaves and 2 tablespoons of butter. Add a cup of warm water and stir. Cook the bhaji for another 10 to 12 minutes over low heat. Season to taste with salt and finish with lemon juice and fresh coriander leaves.
4. Heat the rest of the butter on a pan over low heat and allow it to bubble. Toast the pav for 1 to 2 minutes and serve hot with bhaji, chopped onion, and wedges of lime.

MAHARASHTRA

Kanda Bhajiya

Crispy, spiced onion fritters

Time taken: 25 minutes | Serves 2-3

Ingredients

½ cup chickpea flour
½ teaspoon turmeric powder
1 teaspoon red chilli powder
Salt, to taste
½ teaspoon carom seeds
1 cup thinly sliced onion
1 tablespoon water, if needed
Sunflower or any neutral oil for frying

Method

1. Sift the chickpea flour into a bowl with turmeric and red chilli powders and salt. Add the carom seeds and stir well.
2. Mix the sliced onions with the flour to coat evenly. Set aside to rest for 5 to 10 minutes; the salt in the batter will allow the onions to release their natural moisture, making the mixture sticky. Add a tablespoon of water if needed.
3. Heat the oil in a deep pan over medium heat. Take handfuls of onion and squeeze gently before dropping them into the oil. Fry the bhajiyas until golden brown and drain on kitchen towels.
4. Serve with a chutney or sauce of your choice.

WEST BENGAL

Railway Cutlet

Mixed vegetable patties, generously spiced and crumb-fried

Time taken: 35 minutes | Serves 2-3

Ingredients

¼ cup corn flour
1 tablespoon oil
1 green chilli, finely chopped
½ teaspoon turmeric powder
1 teaspoon red chilli powder
1 teaspoon garam masala
¼ cup finely chopped carrot
½ cup finely chopped beetroot
¼ cup finely chopped French beans
¼ cup peas, boiled
Salt and black pepper, to taste
1 cup boiled and mashed potato
1 tablespoon lemon juice
1 tablespoon finely chopped coriander leaves
Sunflower or any neutral oil for frying
½ cup breadcrumbs

Method

1. **Make the corn flour slurry,** by mixing corn flour with 1 to 2 tablespoons of water. Set aside until needed.
2. **For the cutlet,** heat the oil in a pan over medium heat and add the chopped green chilli. Sauté for a few minutes before stirring in the turmeric and red chilli powders, and garam masala. Add the carrot, beetroot, beans, and peas and season with salt and pepper. Continue to cook until the vegetables soften; add the mashed potato. Cook for another minute and turn off the heat. Add lemon juice and coriander leaves. Mix well.
3. Heat the oil in a deep pan over medium heat and ready the corn flour slurry and breadcrumbs in separate bowls.
4. Take a spoonful of the cutlet mixture and pat it into shape using a cookie cutter. Continue doing this until you have finished all the mix.
5. Dip each cutlet into the corn flour slurry and dredge through the breadcrumbs before frying in hot oil. Drain on kitchen towels. Serve hot with chutney.

STREET FOODS OF INDIA 117

PUNJAB

Amritsari Macchi

Fish marinated in North Indian spices, deep fried

Time taken: 25 minutes | Serves 4-6

Ingredients
Juice of 1 lemon
1 tablespoon ginger–garlic paste
1 teaspoon carom seeds
1 teaspoon red chilli powder
1 teaspoon turmeric powder
1 pinch ground asafoetida
1 tablespoon chickpea flour
Salt, to taste
1 teaspoon rice flour
2 sole fillets
Sunflower or any neutral oil for frying
1 teaspoon chaat masala (page 166)

Method
1. **To make the marinade for the fish,** mix the lemon juice in a bowl with ginger–garlic paste, carom seeds, red chilli and turmeric powders, asafoetida, chickpea flour, a little salt, and rice flour.
2. Coat the fish fillets and allow them to marinate for 10 minutes. Heat the oil in a deep pan over medium heat.
3. Season the fish once more and place the fillets in the pan. Deep fry until golden on both sides. Use a slotted spoon and drain on kitchen towels.
4. Sprinkle with chaat masala and serve hot with mint–coriander chutney (page 168).

TAMIL NADU

Sundal

Chickpeas stir-fried with fresh coconut and spices

Time taken: 10 minutes | Serves 2

Ingredients
½ tablespoon oil
1 teaspoon mustard seeds
1 teaspoon split black lentils
3-4 curry leaves
1 dried red chilli
¼ teaspoon asafoetida
1 cup boiled chickpeas
½ cup freshly grated coconut
Salt, to taste

Method
1. Heat the oil in a pan over medium heat and add a teaspoon of mustard seeds and another of spilt black lentils. Once they begin to crackle, add the curry leaves, red chilli, and asafoetida. Sauté for 30 seconds.
2. Add the boiled chickpeas. Cook for another 3 to 4 minutes and add the grated coconut. Toss well and cook for another minute.
3. Spoon into bowls and serve hot.

STREET FOODS OF INDIA 119

TAMIL NADU

Atho

Street-style noodles tossed with vegetables and spices

Time taken: 30 minutes | Serves 1-2

Ingredients
4 dry red chillies
3 tablespoons peanuts
1½ cups chickpea flour
3 tablespoons shredded onion
½ cup finely sliced cabbage
Salt, to taste
1 pinch sugar
Juice of ½ lemon
3 tablespoons tamarind paste
1 cup cooked noodles of choice
1 teaspoon red chilli powder
½ teaspoon rice flour
1 tablespoon fried onion
3 tablespoons roughly chopped garlic, fried
2 thattai or nippattu, crushed (available at grocery stores)

Method
1. Heat a pan over medium heat and dry roast the red chillies until fragrant. Once cool, grind them into a powder.
2. In another pan over low heat, dry roast the peanuts and crush them in a mortar and pestle.
3. In the same pan, roast the chickpea flour over low heat for a few minutes.
4. Combine the raw onion and finely sliced cabbage in a bowl. Season with salt, sugar, lemon juice, and tamarind paste. Mix well with your fingers and set aside for 10 minutes. Transfer to a wide serving bowl.
5. Add the cooked noodles, red chilli powder, rice flour, fried onion and garlic, crushed peanuts, roasted chickpea flour, and thattai or nippattu.
6. Season to taste with salt and serve immediately.

NORTH INDIA

Mountain Maggi

India's most popular instant noodles, with an Indian twist

Time taken: 25 minutes | Serves 2

Ingredients
1 tablespoon butter
1 teaspoon minced green chilli
1 teaspoon ginger–garlic paste
½ teaspoon turmeric powder
1 teaspoon red chilli powder
¼ cup finely chopped onion
¼ cup finely chopped tomato
¼ cup finely chopped capsicum
3 tablespoons boiled green peas
1 packet instant Maggi noodles
2 cups water
1 teaspoon garam masala
1 teaspoon chaat masala (page 166)
Salt, to taste
1 tablespoon finely chopped coriander leaves

Method
1. Heat the butter in a saucepan over medium heat and add the minced green chilli and ginger–garlic paste. Sauté for a minute before adding the turmeric and red chilli powders. Stir well and tip in the finely chopped onion. Continue to cook until the onions are translucent, (3 to 4 minutes).
2. Stir in the finely chopped tomato and capsicum, and cook until the vegetables soften (3 to 4 minutes).
3. Add the green peas along with Maggi noodles to the masala with 2 cups water to cook the noodles. Once the noodles have cooked, (3 to 4 minutes), stir in the garam masala and chaat masala. Season to taste with salt.
4. Ladle into wide bowls and garnish with coriander leaves. Serve hot.

STREET FOODS OF INDIA 121

MAHARASHTRA

Vada Pav

Bombay's favourite burger

Time taken: 30 minutes | Serves 4

Ingredients

1 tablespoon sunflower or any neutral oil
1 teaspoon mustard seeds
4 curry leaves
1 pinch asafoetida
1 tablespoon minced garlic
1 teaspoon turmeric powder
1 teaspoon red chilli powder
1 teaspoon garam masala
1 cup boiled and mashed potato
Salt, to taste
Juice of ½ lemon
¼ cup finely chopped coriander leaves
2 cups chickpea flour
1 pinch carom seeds
Sunflower or any neutral oil for frying

4 pieces pav
1 tablespoon red garlic chutney (page 170)

Method

1. **To make the vada filling,** heat the oil in a pan over medium-low heat and add mustard seeds. Once they begin to crackle, add the curry leaves and a pinch of asafoetida. Stir in the minced garlic and sauté for a minute before adding turmeric and red chilli powders, and garam masala. Mix the potatoes into the masala and stir thoroughly. Continue to cook for another 4 to 5 minutes. Add salt, lemon juice, and coriander leaves. Roll spoonsful of the potato into small balls and set aside.

2. Meanwhile sift the chickpea flour with salt and carom seeds and slowly add water until you get a pancake batter-like consistency.

3. Heat the oil in a deep pan or skillet over medium heat for deep frying. Dip each vada ball into the prepared chickpea flour batter and gently drop it into the hot oil. Deep fry until golden-brown and drain on kitchen towels.

4. **To assemble,** slice the pav in half, making sure not to cut through the whole piece. You want the pav to flip open. Sprinkle garlic chutney onto the pav and place a vada on top. Close the 'lid' of the pav and serve hot.

TAMIL NADU AND ANDHRA PRADESH

Tender Coconut Shake

Milkshake made with tender coconut and coconut milk

Time taken: 30 minutes | Serves 2-3

Ingredients
1 cup coconut flesh
1 pinch cardamom powder
¼ cup milk
½ cup coconut milk, in ice cube form
Sugar, to taste

Method
1. Place the coconut flesh in the jar of a blender along with a pinch of cardamom powder, milk, and the coconut milk ice cubes. Add sugar and blend. Taste and adjust the sugar and cardamom powder as needed.
2. Pour into tall glasses and serve chilled.

GUJARAT

Dakor Na Gota

Deep-fried and spicy fritters

Time taken: 20 minutes | Serves 2-3

Ingredients
1 cup chickpea flour
½ cup semolina
1 pinch baking soda
1 teaspoon garam masala
2 teaspoons red chilli powder
1 teaspoon turmeric powder
1 tablespoon coriander powder
1 teaspoon black pepper powder
2 teaspoons crushed fennel seeds
1 teaspoon cumin seeds
1 tablespoon ginger–garlic paste
2 tablespoons finely chopped coriander leaves
Salt, to taste
Sunflower or any neutral oil for frying

Method
1. Sift the chickpea flour in a bowl with semolina, baking soda, garam masala, red chilli, turmeric, coriander and pepper powders, crushed fennel seeds, and cumin seeds.
2. Add the ginger–garlic paste and coriander leaves. Season to taste with salt. Adding as little water as possible, whisk into a thick batter of dropping consistency.
3. Heat the oil in a deep pan over medium heat.
4. Deep fry a spoonful at a time in very hot oil until the fritter turns golden-brown (3 to 4 minutes). Use a slotted spoon and drain on kitchen towels.
5. Serve hot with a chutney of your choice.

MAHARASHTRA

Bombay Sandwich

A grilled sandwich with fresh vegetables, cheese, and green chutney

Time taken: 15 minutes | Serves 3

Ingredients

FOR THE CHUTNEY
2 cups coriander leaves
3 tablespoons blanched spinach purée
5 ice cubes
6 green chillies
6 garlic cloves
2 teaspoons minced ginger
2 teaspoons chaat masala (page 166)
½ tablespoon chickpea flour
Salt, to taste

FOR THE SANDWICH
6 slices of white bread
3 tablespoons butter
½ cup thinly sliced onion
½ cup boiled and thinly sliced potato
½ cup thinly sliced tomato
½ cup thinly sliced cucumber
½ cup sliced capsicum (optional)
½ cup grated cheese
1 tablespoon chaat masala (page 166)
Salt and black pepper, to taste

Method

1. **To make the chutney**, use a mixer-grinder or food processor to grind the coriander leaves and spinach purée with ice cubes, green chilli, garlic, minced ginger, chaat masala, and chickpea flour. Blend the ingredients into a fine chutney and set aside.
2. Butter each slice of bread and liberally spread with chutney.
3. **To assemble**, layer three slices of bread with thinly sliced onion, potato, tomato, cucumber, and capsicum. Generously grate cheese over the vegetables and sprinkle with chaat masala, salt, and black pepper. Cover with the other slices of bread.
4. Butter each sandwich on both sides from the outside and grill in a sandwich maker. You can also grill the sandwiches on a grill pan, carefully turning them once to achieve an even char on the bread.
5. Cut into triangles and serve hot with chilli sauce, tomato ketchup, or mint–coriander chutney (page 168).

STREET FOODS OF INDIA 125

PUNJAB

Paneer Tikka

Spicy marinated cottage cheese skewers

Time taken: 55 minutes | Serves 2-3

Ingredients

½ cup hung curd
1 tablespoon ginger–garlic paste
1 teaspoon chickpea flour
1 teaspoon roasted cumin powder
1 teaspoon dry mango powder
1 tablespoon coriander powder
1 teaspoon red chilli powder
2 teaspoons tikka masala
1 teaspoon garam masala
Salt, to taste
Juice of ½ lemon
1 cup cubed cottage cheese
1 cup diced capsicum
1 cup diced onion
5 tablespoons butter
1 tablespoon ghee
1 tablespoon chaat masala (page 166)

Method

1. Whisk the hung curd with ginger–garlic paste, chickpea flour, cumin, dry mango, coriander and red chilli powders, tikka masala, garam masala and a pinch of salt, and stir well. Season with a dash of lemon juice. Gently toss the paneer, capsicum and onion in the marinade and rest for 40 minutes.
2. Thread paneer, capsicum and onion onto skewers.
3. Heat the butter in a grill pan over medium heat. Brush ghee onto the tikkas.
4. Grill the skewers on all sides until deliciously charred and smoky, about 10 to 12 minutes.
5. Sprinkle chaat masala over the skewers and serve hot.

UTTRAKHAND

Kumaoni Bada

Vegan lentil fritters seasoned with spices

Time taken: 20 minutes | Serves 2-3

Ingredients

1 cup split black lentils, soaked overnight
1 pinch asafoetida
1 teaspoon red chilli powder
1 teaspoon turmeric powder
1 green chilli, finely chopped
¼ cup finely chopped coriander leaves
Salt, to taste
Mustard, sunflower or any neutral oil for frying

Method

1. **To make the bada**, drain the lentils and combine with asafoetida, red chilli and turmeric powders, green chilli, and coriander leaves. Use a mixer-grinder and grind the ingredients into a thick batter. Season to taste with salt.
2. Heat the oil in a kadhai over medium heat. Drop a spoonful of the batter into the oil and deep fry until golden brown. (You can even create a medu vada-style cavity in the centre by taking a portion of the batter on your palm and making a hole in the centre of each bada.) Drain on kitchen towels.
3. Serve hot with a chutney of your choice.

WEST BENGAL

Kolkata Kathi Roll

Spicy chicken kebabs wrapped in a paratha

Time taken: 1 hour 20 minutes | Serves 4

Ingredients

FOR THE GARAM MASALA
1 tablespoon green cardamom
1 teaspoon cloves
1 small piece cinnamon

FOR THE PARATHA
2 cups refined flour
½ teaspoon sugar
1 pinch salt
2 tablespoons ghee
Water as needed

FOR THE FILLING
2 tablespoons yoghurt
1 tablespoon red chilli powder
1 tablespoon ginger–garlic paste
Juice of ½ lemon
3 teaspoons garam moshala, divided
1 cup cubed boneless chicken
1 tablespoon mustard oil
1 teaspoon ghee
½ cup sliced green capsicum
½ cup sliced onion
Salt, to taste

FOR THE GARNISH
1 onion, sliced
1 green chilli, finely chopped
1 teaspoon chaat masala (page 166)
1 teaspoon lemon juice

Method

1. **To make the garam masala,** dry roast the cardamom, cloves, and cinnamon stick in a pan before pounding them to a fine powder in a mortar and pestle. Keep aside.
2. **To make the garnish,** in a small bowl, mix the sliced onion with finely chopped green chilli, a teaspoon of chaat masala and a squeeze of lemon juice, and set aside until needed.
3. **To make the paratha,** sift the flour with half a teaspoon of sugar and a pinch of salt. Rub ghee into the flour with your fingertips until it resembles coarse sand. Adding water a few drops at a time, knead into a soft dough. Cover the bowl with a moist muslin cloth and allow the dough to rest for 30 minutes.
4. Meanwhile, whisk the yoghurt with red chilli powder, ginger–garlic paste, lemon juice, and 2 teaspoons of the fresh garam masala. Toss the cubed chicken in the marinade and set aside for 30 minutes. If you would like to smoke the meat, you may do so at this stage. (see page 101).
5. Preheat the oven at 220 degrees C.
6. Skewer the marinated chicken cubes on sticks and baste with mustard oil. Place the skewers on a rimmed baking sheet and bake until the chicken is cooked through, about 15 minutes.
7. While the chicken is cooking, heat the ghee in a griddle over medium heat. Add the sliced capsicum and onion to the pan along with a teaspoon of garam masala and cook until the vegetables are slightly charred. This should take 3 to 4 minutes. Add the cooked chicken pieces to the pan and toss them together. Season to taste with salt.
8. **To assemble,** place a spoon of filling to the centre of each paratha. Top with the marinated onion mixture and roll into a tight cigar. Serve hot.

KASHMIR

Kashmiri Mutton Tujj

Minced mutton skewers marinated with Kashmiri spice mix

Time taken: 1 hour 30 minutes + 6 hours resting | Serves 1

Ingredients

FOR THE TUJJ MASALA
2 tablespoons cumin seeds
2 tablespoons coriander seeds
2 black cardamoms
5 green cardamoms
1-2 cloves
½ teaspoon carom seeds
2 tablespoons black peppercorns
2 pieces whole mace
1 ½ tablespoon dried fenugreek leaves
1 ½ tablespoon Kashmiri chilli powder
1 tablespoon red chilli powder
1 tablespoon ginger powder
1 tablespoon black salt

2 tablespoons yoghurt
2 tablespoons tujj masala
2 teaspoons Kashmiri red chilli powder
1 teaspoon turmeric powder
1 tablespoon garlic paste
1 cup cubed boneless mutton
Salt, to taste
2 tablespoons oil

Method

1. Roast the cumin and coriander seeds, black and green cardamoms, cloves, carom seeds, peppercorns, and mace in a pan over low heat for 2 to 3 minutes, till the spices release a faint aroma. Remove from heat. Once the roasted spices have cooled, put them in the jar of a masala grinder along with the dried fenugreek leaves, Kashmiri chilli powder, red chilli and ginger powders, and black salt. Blitz to a fine powder. This is the tujj masala.
2. Whisk the yoghurt in a bowl with the tujj masala, Kashmiri chilli and turmeric powders, and garlic paste. Add the mutton pieces and season with salt. Refrigerate the marinade for a least 6 hours, preferably overnight.
3. Take the marinated meat out of the fridge at least 45 minutes before you want to cook it to allow it to reach room temperature. Thread the mutton onto skewers and brush with oil.
4. Cook the skewers on an open flame or a grill until the mutton is cooked; about 17-20 minutes. You can also cook the skewers in an oven at 200 degrees C for 20 minutes. Preheat the oven while you are threading the mutton onto skewers.
5. Serve with mint–coriander chutney (page 168) and sliced onion.

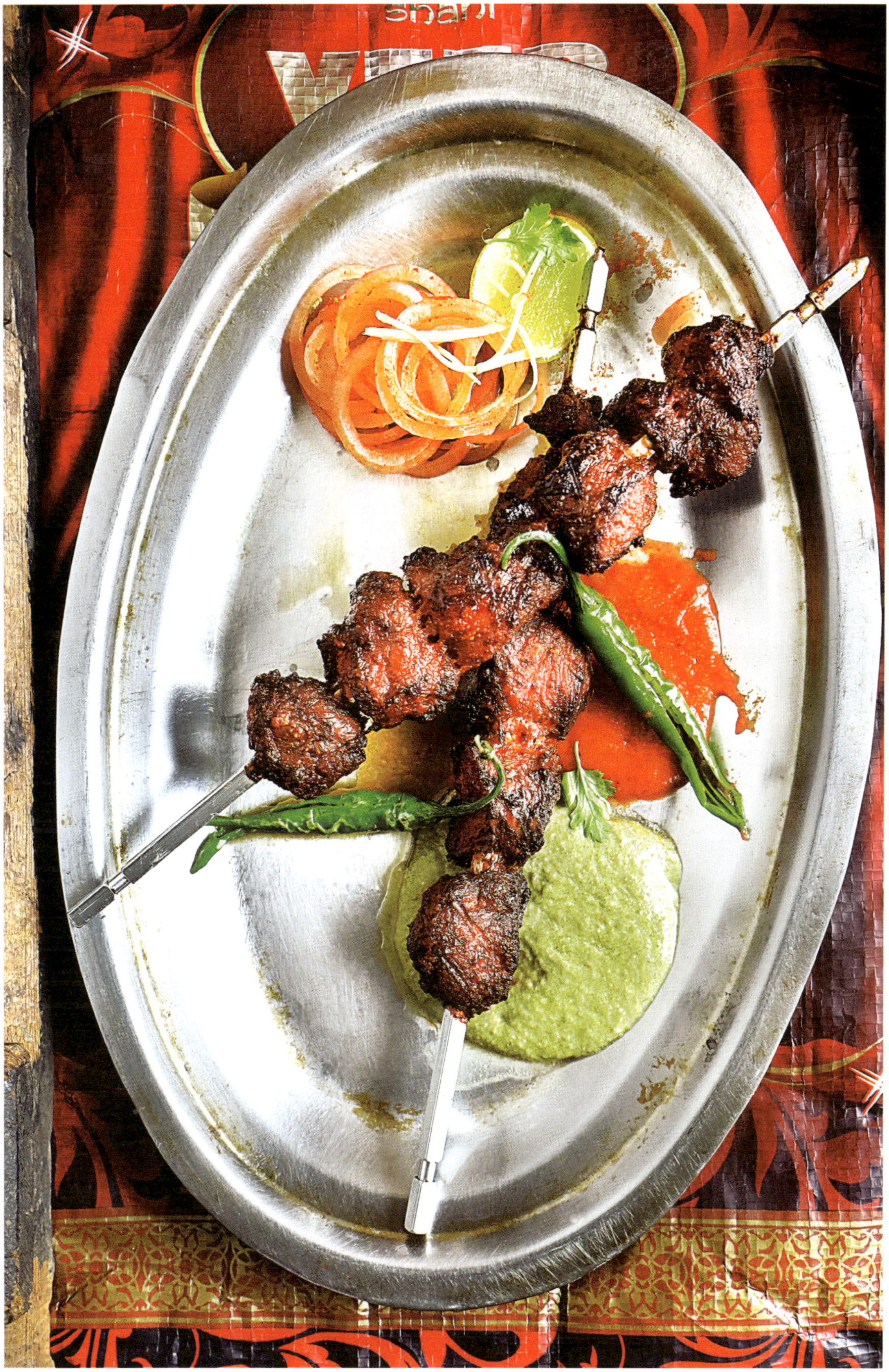

MANIPUR

Paknam

Fish and leeks cooked in turmeric leaves

Time taken: 35 minutes | Serves 2-3

Ingredients
¾ cup finely chopped winter leek
5 to 6 ngari fish (fermented fish) (available online)
1 green chilli, finely chopped
¾ cup chickpea flour
Salt, to taste
3 to 4 turmeric leaves

Method
1. Crush the chopped leek with your hands for a few minutes and add to a bowl. Add the ngari fish, finely chopped green chilli, and chickpea flour. Continue to crush gently until it forms a rough paste. Season to taste with salt. Add a few drops of water if it does not bind well.
2. Once you have a thick paste you are ready to cook the paknam.
3. Lay the turmeric leaves on the kitchen counter and scoop the batter into the centre of the leaves and gently pat it into a square shape. Fold the turmeric leaves and create a square or rectangular parcel with the batter in the middle. Tie the leaves using a cooking string. You may make multiple parcels; each should have approximately ½ cup of the batter.
4. Pressure cook the paknam with 2 cups of water for 3 whistles. Once the pressure has cooled, cook the parcels on a hot griddle for 3 to 4 minutes, until the leaves have charred nicely.
5. Open the leaves and cut the paknam into squares. Serve with mint–coriander chutney (page 168).

MADHYA PRADESH

Egg Banjo

Spicy omelette sandwiched between buns

Time taken: 15 minutes | Serves 2

Ingredients
2 eggs
¼ cup finely chopped coriander leaves
1 teaspoon cumin seeds
1 teaspoon minced ginger
1 teaspoon red chilli powder
1 green chilli, finely chopped
Salt, to taste
2 teaspoons vegetable oil
1 tablespoon butter
2 burger buns, sliced
½ cup sliced onion
1 tomato, sliced
2 tablespoons tomato ketchup

Method
1. In a medium-size bowl, whisk the eggs with coriander leaves, cumin seeds, minced ginger, red chilli powder, and finely chopped green chilli. Season to taste with salt.
2. Heat the oil in a skillet over medium heat.
3. Pour half the egg batter into the skillet and spread it evenly. Cook on both sides until golden brown. Remove and set aside. Repeat with the remaining egg batter to make another omelette.
4. Butter half of each bun and place an omelette on top. Layer with onion and tomato slices. Spread ketchup on the other halves of the buns and close the sandwiches.
5. Cut the burgers in half and serve with mint–coriander chutney (page 168).

NORTH INDIA

Egg Tikka

Smoky, marinated egg skewers

Time taken: 25 minutes | Serves 4

Ingredients

¼ cup finely chopped onion
1 green chilli, finely chopped
1 cup diced green and red capsicum
1 tablespoon finely chopped coriander leaves
1 teaspoon minced ginger
1 teaspoon red chilli powder
1 teaspoon coriander powder
1 teaspoon garam masala
5 eggs
Salt and black pepper, to taste
1 tablespoon butter
¼ cup diced onion
¼ cup diced capsicum

FOR THE MARINADE
1 teaspoon vegetable oil
¾ cup thick yoghurt
2 tablespoons chickpea flour
1 teaspoon red chilli powder
1 teaspoon coriander powder
1 teaspoon cumin powder
1 teaspoon garam masala
1 tablespoon ginger–garlic paste
1 tablespoon tikka masala
Salt, to taste
1 teaspoon black pepper powder
1 teaspoon chaat masala (page 166)

Method

1. Mix the finely chopped onions with green chilli, diced capsicums, coriander leaves, minced ginger, red chilli and coriander powders, and garam masala. In a separate bowl, whisk the eggs and add the vegetable mixture to it. Combine well to form a thick batter. Season to taste with salt and pepper.
2. Heat the butter in a pan over low heat and pour the egg batter into it. Cook the egg like a frittata for 6 to 7 minutes until just done.
3. Cut the frittata into thick squares.
4. **To make the marinade**, whisk the yoghurt with chickpea flour, red chilli, coriander, and cumin powders, garam masala, ginger–garlic paste, tikka masala, salt, and black pepper. Mix in the egg cubes, diced onion and capsicum.
5. Alternately, thread egg, capsicum and onion onto skewers while you heat oil in a grill pan over medium heat. Brush oil onto the skewers.
6. Grill the skewers on all sides until deliciously charred and smoky, about 2 to 3 minutes per side
7. Sprinkle chaat masala over the skewers and serve hot.

STREET FOODS OF INDIA 133

MAHARASHTRA

Bhindi Bazaar Seekh Kebab

Tender minced meat skewers

Time taken: 45 minutes | Serves 2-3

Ingredients
1 cup minced mutton
1 tablespoon ginger–garlic paste
¼ cup finely chopped coriander leaves
3 tablespoons finely chopped mint leaves
1 green chilli, finely chopped
1 teaspoon turmeric powder
2 teaspoons garam masala
Salt, to taste
1 teaspoon black pepper powder
1 onion, minced
1 tablespoon chickpea flour
5 tablespoon sunflower or any neutral oil

TO SERVE
Green chilli–coriander chutney (page 170)
Wedges of lime
1 onion, thinly sliced rounds

Method
1. Using your hands, gently mix the minced mutton with ginger–garlic paste, coriander and mint leaves, green chilli, turmeric powder, garam masala, salt, and pepper.
2. Wrap the minced onion in a muslin cloth and squeeze out all the water. Add to the mutton along with a tablespoon of chickpea flour. Mix well, but do not overwork the mince. Cover and rest for 30 minutes.
3. Set a grill pan to heat over medium heat and prepare skewers for the seekh kebab.
4. Wetting your palms, press the mince onto each skewer in the shape of a sausage, approximately 4 to 5 inches long. Brush with oil. Place the skewers over the pan and cook for 18 to 20 minutes on each side until the kebabs are done.
5. Serve hot with green chilli–coriander chutney, wedges of lime, and slices of onion.

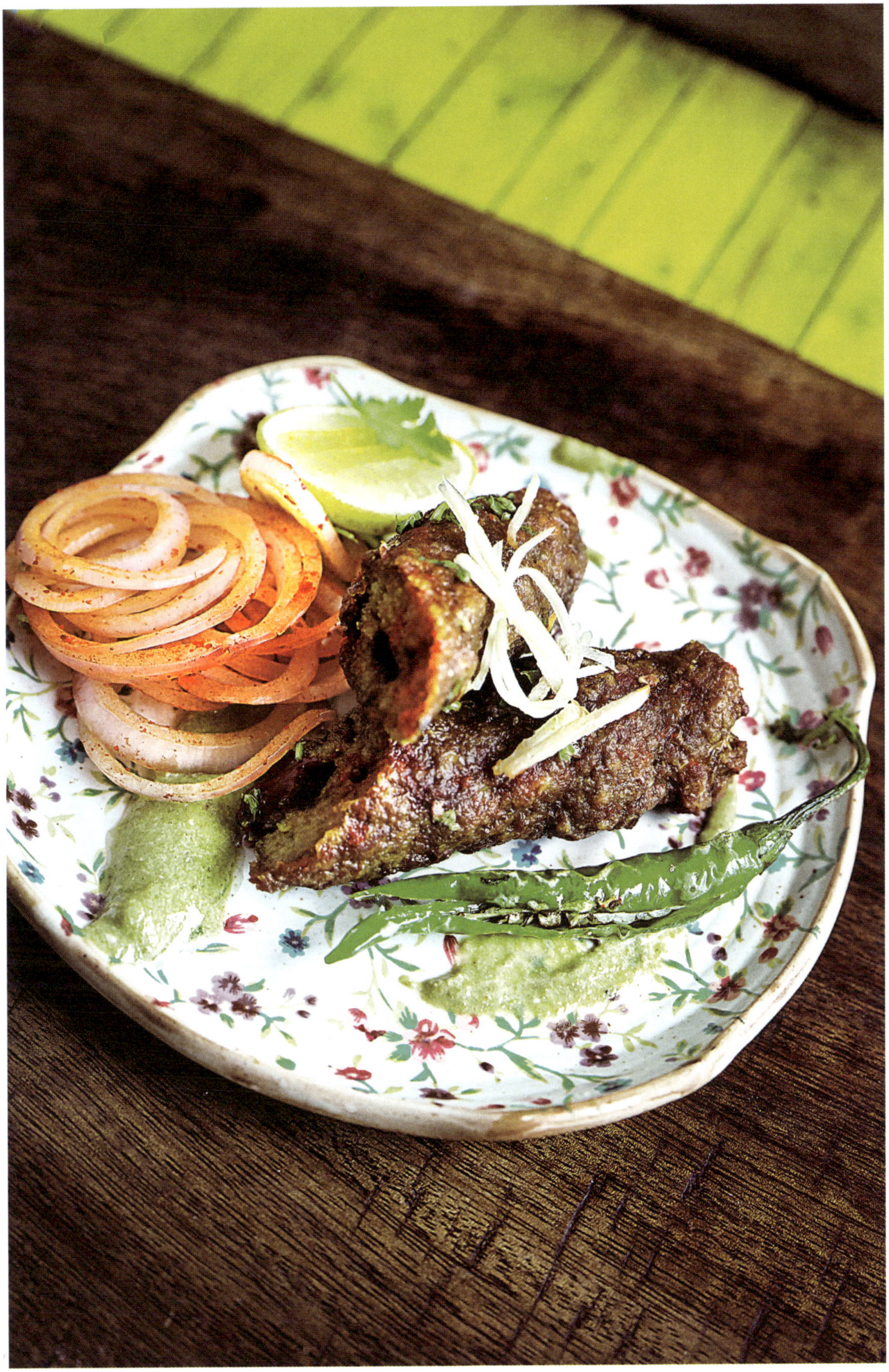

PAN-INDIA

Chicken Shawarma

Pita bread stuffed with chicken, pickled vegetables, and garlic sauce

Time taken: 1 hour 30 minutes | Serves 4

Ingredients

FOR THE PICKLE
½ cup batons beetroot
½ cup batons carrot
½ cup batons radish
1 green chilli, finely chopped
1 cup vinegar
1 teaspoon salt
4 teaspoons sugar
½ cup water

FOR THE PITA BREAD
1 teaspoon sugar
1 teaspoon instant dried yeast
½ cup lukewarm milk
1¼ cups refined flour
1 teaspoon oil
Pinch of salt
Lukewarm water to knead
1 tablespoon black sesame seeds
4 tablespoons butter

FOR THE GARLIC SAUCE (TOUM)
½ cup peeled garlic
1½ cup sunflower or any neutral oil
1 tablespoon lemon juice
Salt, to taste

FOR THE CHICKEN FILLING
¼ cup thick yoghurt
1 tablespoon ginger–garlic paste
1 tablespoon lemon juice
2 teaspoons red chilli powder
2 teaspoons cumin powder
2 teaspoons coriander powder
2 teaspoons garam masala
Salt, to taste
3 fillets boneless chicken
1 tablespoon butter

TO SERVE
½ cup finely sliced onions
½ cup shredded cabbage
1 cup French fries
¼ cup hot sauce of choice
Juice of 1 lemon

Method

1. **Make the pickle** first to allow it to intensify in flavour. Blanch the beetroot, carrot and radish in hot water for 3 to 4 minutes. Drain the vegetables in a colander and place them under running water for a minute to cool.
2. Meanwhile, mix half a cup of water in a jar with green chilli, vinegar, salt, and sugar. Shake well and add the blanched vegetables to the jar. Cover and allow it to rest for at least 45 minutes.
3. **To make the pita**, sprinkle the instant yeast and sugar in a bowl with half a cup of lukewarm milk. Stir and leave aside for 8 to 10 minutes. While the yeast is activating, knead the flour with a teaspoon of oil, a pinch of salt, and a little water to form a rough dough. Add the milk and yeast to the flour and knead into a soft dough, adding more water if needed. Cover the bowl with a damp muslin cloth and allow to rest for 30 minutes.
4. Dab oil all over the dough and break into medium-sized balls. Roll each ball into elongated discs and sprinkle with sesame seeds. Heat a griddle or cast iron tava over medium heat. Cook the pita bread for 3 to 4 minutes on each side so they puff up. Spread with butter and set aside.
5. Whisk the yoghurt in a bowl with ginger–garlic paste, lemon juice, red chilli, cumin, and coriander powders, garam masala, and salt until smooth. Add the chicken to the marinade and mix well. Allow it to rest for 30 minutes while you make the toum.
6. **To make the toum,** grind the garlic into a smooth paste in a food processor. Pour 1 tablespoon oil at a time into the running food processor and allow it to blend with the paste. Stop periodically and stir through with a spatula. Continue to slowly pour oil until the garlic paste has emulsified and become fluffy. Finish by adding lemon juice and salt.

7. Heat the butter on a grill pan over medium heat and cook the chicken fillets, turning once, until done. This should take 15 to 18 minutes. Shred the chicken into bite-sized pieces with a fork.
8. **To assemble the shawarma**, layer the pita bread with shredded chicken and spoon heaps of toum over it. Top with pickled vegetables, finely sliced onions, and shredded cabbage. Add a dash of hot sauce and a squeeze of lime. Roll into a loose cigar and serve hot. Best served with more toum and pickled vegetables.

◆◇◆◇◆◇◆

NORTH INDIA

Mutton Momos

Dumplings stuffed with minced mutton and mixed vegetables

Time taken: 1 hour | Serves 1-2

Ingredients

FOR THE DOUGH
1 cup refined flour
1 pinch salt
Lukewarm water to knead
1 tablespoon vegetable oil

FOR THE FILLING
1 tablespoon vegetable oil
½ tablespoon minced ginger–garlic
¼ cup finely chopped onion
½ cup minced mutton
¼ cup finely chopped cabbage
¼ cup finely chopped carrot
2 tablespoons finely chopped coriander leaves
2 teaspoons dark soy sauce
1 teaspoon vinegar
Salt, to taste

Method

1. **To make the dough**, sift the flour with salt. Adding water slowly, knead it into a tight dough. Drizzle the dough with oil and cover the bowl with a damp muslin cloth. Let the dough rest for 40 minutes while you make the filling.
2. Heat the oil in a pan over medium heat and add the ginger–garlic mince. Sauté for a minute before adding the onions. Cook for 2 to 3 minutes, until the onions become translucent. Add the mutton mince. Sauté for 5 to 6 minutes and add the finely chopped cabbage, carrot, and coriander leaves. Cook for another 5 to 6 minutes, until the mince is completely cooked. Add the dark soy sauce and vinegar. Season to taste with salt.
3. Make 3 to 5 balls out of the dough and roll each into a thin circle of 1–2 mm thickness. Using a cookie cutter, cut 7 to 9 palm-sized circles, approximately 3-inch diameter.
4. Place a spoonful of the mince filling in the centre of each circle and bring the edges together. Pinch the momos closed in the centre.
5. Prepare the steamer.
6. Steam the momos for 8 to 10 minutes. Eat them as is or pan-fry them in hot oil for 3 to 4 minutes until the base is crisp. Serve hot with momo chutney (page 172).

SIKKIM

Sha Phaley

Tibetan empanada stuffed with spicy minced meat

Time taken: 45 minutes | Serves 2

Ingredients

½ cup minced mutton
¼ cup finely chopped spring onion, along with the greens
2 tablespoons finely chopped cabbage
1 tablespoon garlic paste
1 tablespoon light soy sauce
1 teaspoon black pepper powder
Salt, to taste
½ cup refined flour
Water to knead
Sunflower or any neutral oil for frying

Method

1. In a bowl, using your hands, gently mix the mutton with chopped onion, cabbage, garlic paste, soy sauce, black pepper, and salt. Cover the bowl and allow the mutton mixture to rest for half an hour.
2. While it is resting, mix the flour with water and knead into a medium-hard dough. Break pieces of the dough and roll them into palm-sized circles.
3. Heat the oil in a deep pan over medium heat.
4. Place a spoonful of the marinated mutton mince on one side of each circle. Fold into half and pinch the corners of the circle closed, carefully pinching and folding like an empanada.
5. In batches, deep fry the mutton parcels over medium heat until golden brown. Use a slotted spoon and drain on kitchen towels.
6. Serve hot with red garlic chutney (page 170).

STREET FOODS OF INDIA 139

TAMIL NADU

Muttai Kalaki
Soft scrambled eggs with korma gravy

Time taken: 10 minutes | Serves 2

Ingredients
2 eggs
1 tablespoon korma gravy of choice
1 pinch chaat masala (page 166)
½ teaspoon black pepper powder
Salt, to taste
1 teaspoon oil

Method
1. In a bowl, whisk the egg until frothy and add a tablespoon of korma gravy to it. This can be any leftover gravy you have. Whisk to combine and add chaat masala and pepper. Season to taste with salt.
2. Heat the oil in a pan over medium heat and wait until the oil gets very hot. Pour the egg into the centre of the pan.
3. The moment the egg batter is placed in the pan, use a silicon spatula, and begin folding the 'omelette' inwards, creating a blob in the centre. Cook for 5 to 10 seconds only, do not allow it to cook fully.
4. Once the outer layer is cooked, remove from the pan, and serve hot.

BIHAR

Bihari Kebab
Spicy chicken skewers

Time taken: 45 minutes + 5 hours resting | Serves 2-3

Ingredients
½ cup finely sliced onion, fried and blended to a paste
5 tablespoons hung curd
1 tablespoon ginger–garlic paste
1 tablespoon coriander powder
2 teaspoons cumin powder
2 teaspoons red chilli powder
½ teaspoon mace powder
1 pinch star anise powder
Salt, to taste
Sunflower or any neutral oil for frying
1 cup cubed boneless chicken
2 tablespoons ghee

TO SERVE
Green chilli–coriander chutney (page 170)
Wedges of lime
1 onion, sliced

Method
1. Whisk the fried onion paste in a bowl with the hung curd, ginger–garlic paste, coriander, cumin, red chilli, mace, and star anise powders until smooth. Season to taste with salt.
2. Add the chicken pieces to the marinade and mix well. Refrigerate for 4 to 5 hours and remove from the fridge 45 minutes before you are ready to cook and allow it to reach to room temperature.
3. Thread the chicken onto skewers while you heat the oil in a grill pan over medium heat. Place the chicken skewers on the grill pan and cook, rotating frequently to keep it from burning. Baste occasionally with ghee. The chicken will take between 20 and 25 minutes to cook.
4. Serve hot with green chilli–coriander chutney, wedges of lime, and slices of onion.

📍 UTTAR PRADESH

Keema Baida Roti

Minced meat stuffed square wraps

Time taken: 30 minutes + 2 hours resting | Serves 2-3

Ingredients

FOR THE ROTI
1 cup refined flour
1 teaspoon sunflower or any neutral oil
1 pinch salt

FOR THE FILLING
½ cup oil
1 cup keema stuffing (step 5, page 101)
½ cup finely chopped onion
1 green chilli, finely chopped
4 eggs, whisked
Salt, to taste

TO SERVE
Green chilli–coriander chutney (page 170)
Wedges of lime
1 onion, thinly sliced

Method

1. **To make the rotis**, knead the flour with a teaspoon of oil and a pinch of salt until you have a soft dough. Cover the bowl with a damp muslin cloth and allow the dough to rest for 2 hours.
2. Portion the dough into medium-sized balls.
3. Roll the dough balls into large rotis, larger than you would normally roll them, making sure the rotis are thin. The rotis do not need to be perfectly round, in fact, a square shape is preferred. Brush the rotis with oil on both sides.
4. Heat the oil in a skillet over medium heat.
5. Place 2 large spoonsful of keema in the centre of each roti, and top with some onion and green chilli. Pour a large spoonful of the whisked egg over the keema and season to taste with salt. Quickly fold the roti from all four sides, like an envelope.
6. Shallow fry the roti until crisp and golden on both sides. This will take about 7 to 9 minutes. Drain on kitchen towels.
7. Cut the roti into squares and serve with green chilli–coriander chutney, wedges of lime, and slices of onion.

UNIQUE CHAATS FROM MY KITCHEN

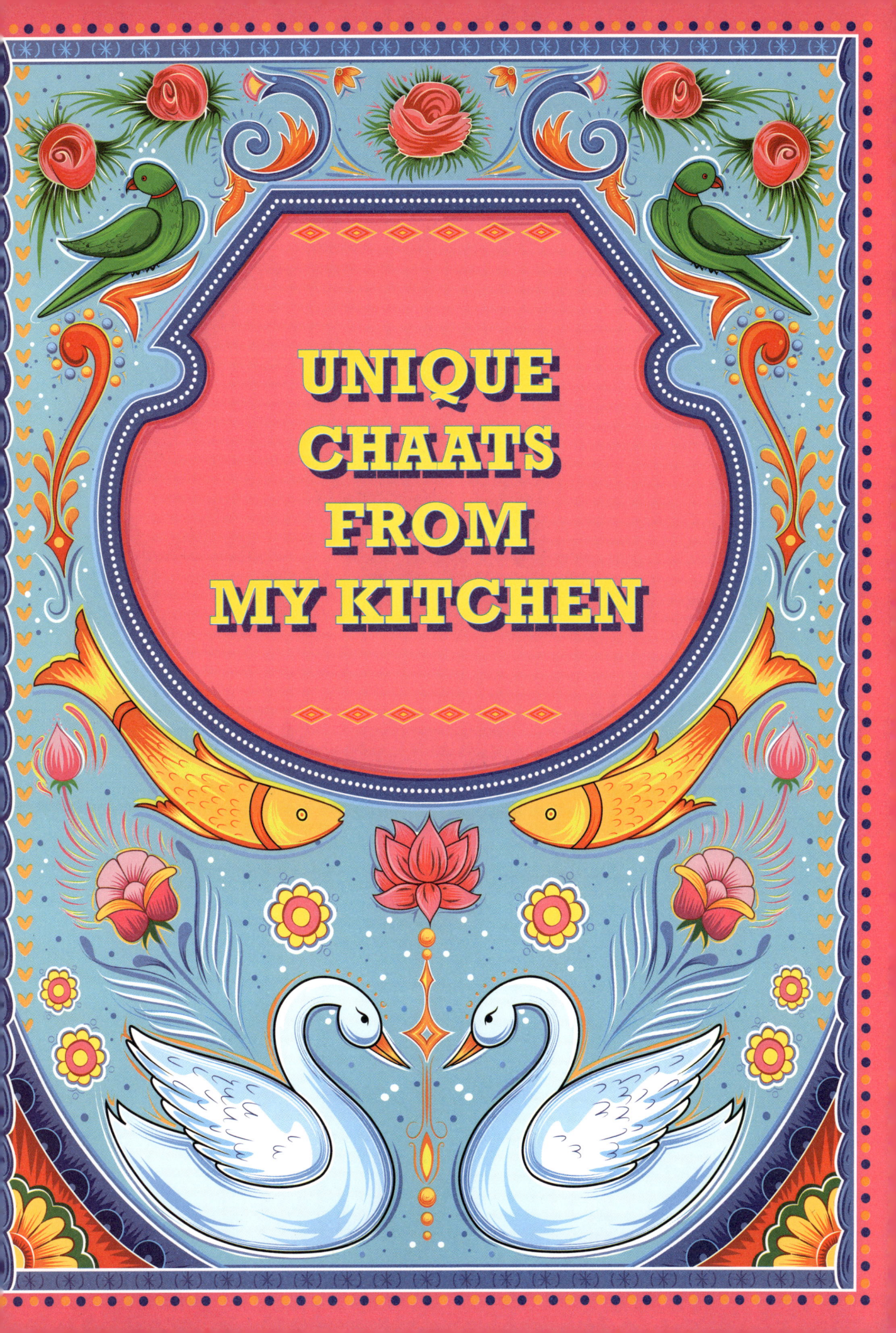

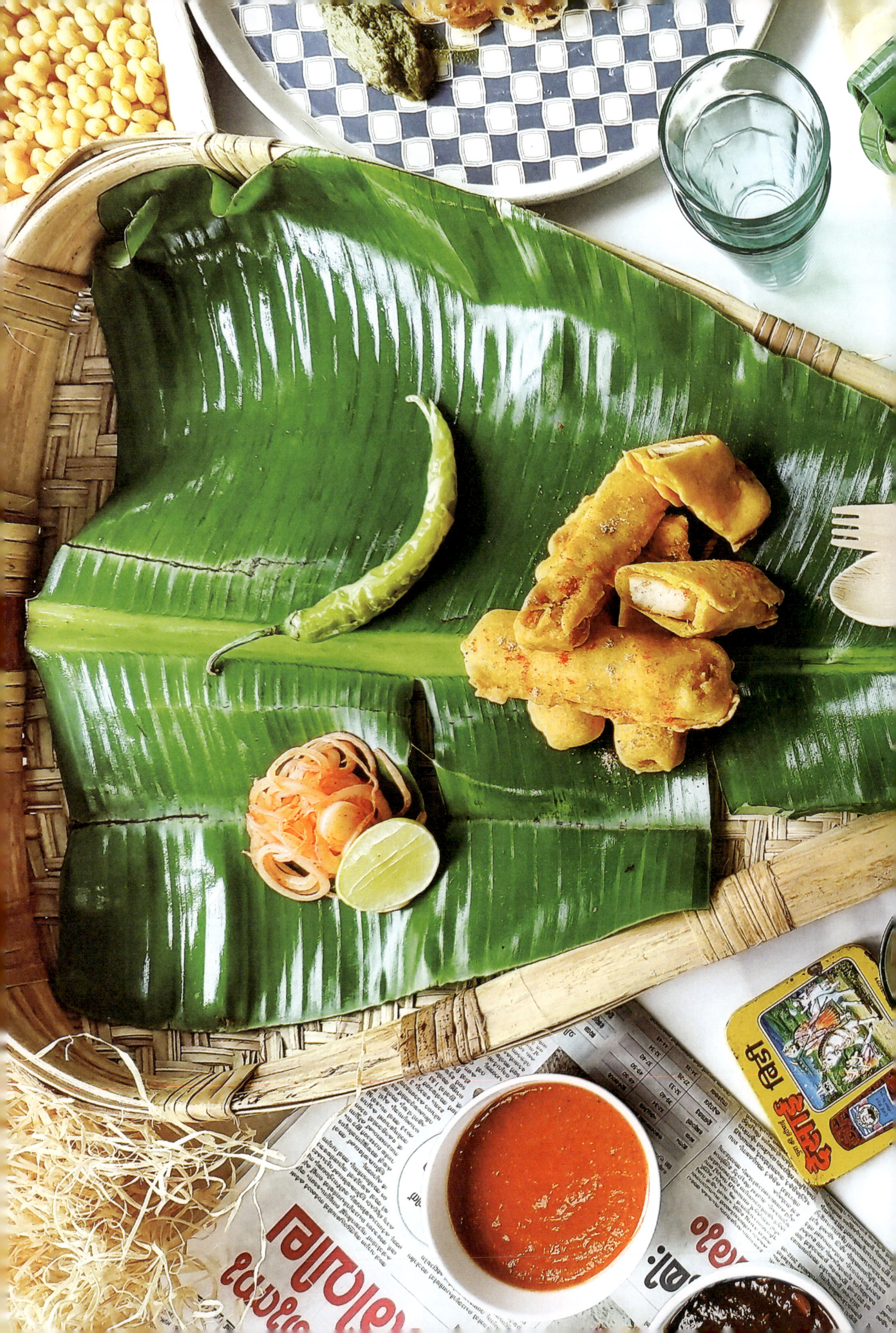

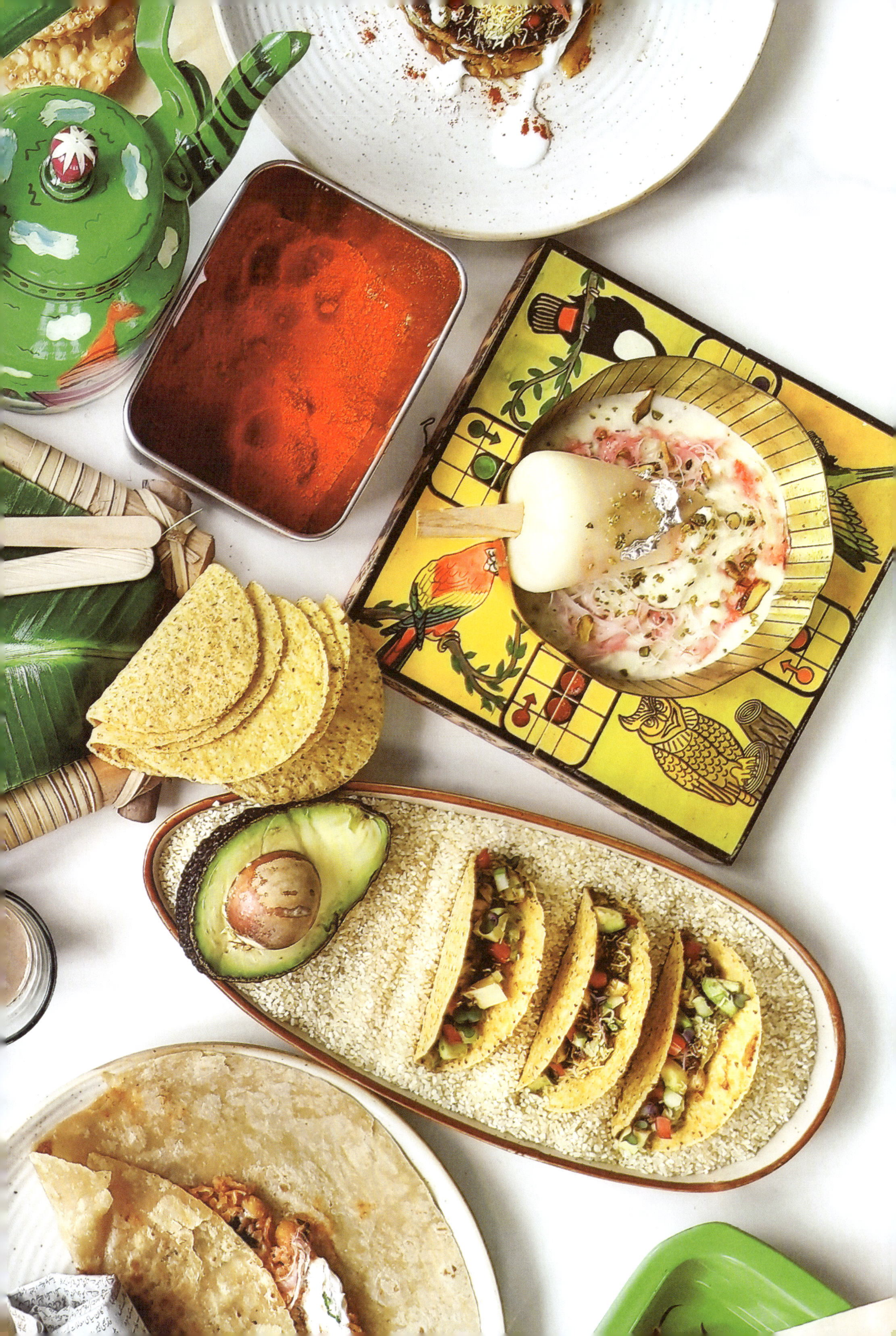

Cheesy Paneer Cone Chaat

Vegetables and cottage cheese served in a waffle cone

Time taken: 10 minutes | Serves 2

Ingredients

1 teaspoon vegetable oil
1 teaspoon tandoori masala
1 tablespoon diced cottage cheese
Salt, to taste
2 tablespoons mayonnaise
2 waffle cones
¼ cup green chilli–coriander chutney (page 170)
2 tablespoons ragda (page 71)
1 cup boiled corn
¼ cup finely chopped tomato
¼ cup finely chopped onion
¼ cup tamarind–jaggery chutney (page 169)
1 tablespoon crushed papdi (page 174)
1 tablespoon grated cheese
1 tablespoon fresh coriander leaves
1 lemon, halved
1 tablespoon chaat masala (page 166)

Method

1. Heat the oil in a small pan over medium heat and add the tandoori masala. Allow to cook for a minute before adding the cottage cheese. Toss well making sure the masala is coated evenly. Season to taste with salt.
2. Spread a generous dollop of mayonnaise on the walls of each waffle cone and repeat with green chilli–coriander chutney.
3. Spoon the ragda into the bottom of each cone and layer with boiled corn, finely chopped onion and tomato, cooked cottage cheese, tamarind–jaggery chutney, crushed papdi, grated cheese, and fresh coriander leaves.
4. Squeeze lemon juice and sprinkle some chaat masala on top and serve.

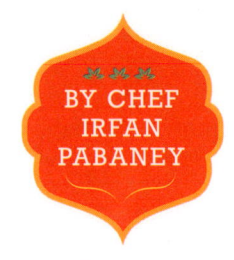

BY CHEF IRFAN PABANEY

UNIQUE CHAATS FROM MY KITCHEN 147

Pani Puri with Asian Slaw and Fragrant Herb Water

An Asian twist on a classic favourite

Time taken: 25 minutes | Serves 4

Ingredients

FOR THE PANI
1 tablespoon butter
2 cups sliced fresh pineapple
2 teaspoons roasted cumin powder
1 teaspoon ginger paste
½ cup pineapple juice
1 green chilli
Black salt, to taste
½ cup basil leaves
¼ cup mint leaves
¼ cup finely chopped coriander leaves
1 kafir lime leaf
1 teaspoon dry mango powder
2 teaspoons jaggery powder
2 tablespoons finely chopped mint leaves
Salt and black pepper, to taste

FOR THE FILLING
1 tablespoon finely chopped raw mango
Juice of 1 lemon
1 teaspoon grated ginger
2 teaspoons honey
1 teaspoon sesame oil
2 teaspoons peanuts, ground to powder

FOR THE SLAW
½ cup moong sprouts, soaked overnight and boiled
½ cup finely chopped onion
½ cup finely chopped red capsicum
1 fresh minced red chilli
2 carrots, grated
½ cup shredded coriander leaves
½ cup shredded mint leaves
Salt, to taste

Method

1. **To make the pani,** warm butter in a heavy-bottomed pan and roast the pineapple slices until they are gently charred. Sprinkle the cumin powder and ginger paste on top and toss for a few minutes. Transfer to a blender.
2. Add the pineapple juice, green chilli, basil, mint, coriander, and kafir lime leaves in the blender along with the dry mango and jaggery powders. Blend well and strain into a jug. Season to taste with salt and black pepper and allow the pineapple water to chill in the refrigerator.
3. **To make the filling,** place the chopped raw mango, lemon juice, ginger, honey, sesame oil, and an ice cube in a blender. Blend into a thin dressing.
4. Toss the moong sprouts, onion, red capsicum, minced chilli, grated carrot, coriander and mint leaves in the dressing and season with salt.
5. **To serve,** stuff each puri generously with the filling and serve with chilled pineapple water.

Barley and Couscous Tikki, Mango Cream and Birista

Spicy crumb-fried cakes with mango cream and fried onions

Time taken: 20 minutes | Serves 4

Ingredients

FOR THE TIKKI
½ cup boiled barley
½ cup boiled couscous
½ cup boiled and mashed potato
½ cup boiled and mashed sweet potato
¼ cup finely chopped onion
1 teaspoon black pepper powder
1 tablespoon red chilli powder
1 teaspoon turmeric powder
1½ tablespoons coriander powder
2 teaspoons roasted cumin powder
1 tablespoon ginger–garlic paste
½ cup finely chopped coriander + mint leaves
¼ cup finely sliced onion, fried until crisp (birista)
2 teaspoons chilli sauce of choice
Salt, to taste
Breadcrumbs for binding
Sunflower or any neutral oil for frying

FOR THE MANGO CREAM
3 tablespoons mango pickle
½ cup heavy cream
½ teaspoon black pepper powder

FOR THE GARNISH
¼ cup finely chopped onion
2 tablespoons finely chopped coriander
¼ cup nylon sev
2 tablespoons pomegranate gems

Method

1. **To make the tikki,** combine the barley, couscous, potato, sweet potato and chopped onions in a bowl. Add the black pepper, red chilli, turmeric, coriander and roasted cumin powders, ginger–garlic paste, coriander and mint leaves and bring the mixture together using a potato masher.
2. Add the birista and chilli sauce and stir through. Season to taste with salt and roll into palm-sized tikkis, with breadcrumbs pressing very gently to flatten them.
3. Heat the oil in a skillet over medium heat and shallow fry tikkis until golden brown. Drain on kitchen towels.
4. **To make the mango cream,** blitz the mango pickle and cream together in a blender and season with black pepper.
5. **Plate and serve** the tikkis hot. Top with a few spoons of mango cream, finely chopped onions, coriander, nylon sev, and pomegranate gems.

Papdi 'Lasagna' with Orange Yoghurt

Crispy flour discs layered with cottage cheese, potato, and yoghurt sauce

Time taken: 15 minutes | Serves 4-6

Ingredients

FOR THE ORANGE YOGHURT
1 cup chilled thick yoghurt
½ cup orange juice
1 teaspoon orange zest
Salt, to taste

FOR THE LASAGNA MIXTURE
1 cup grated cottage cheese
1 cup mashed potato
¼ cup finely chopped coriander leaves
¼ cup finely chopped mint leaves
4 tablespoons tamarind pulp
1 tablespoon red chilli powder
1 tablespoon cumin powder
3 teaspoons chaat masala (page 166)
1 tablespoon pomegranate gems
½ cup finely chopped tomato
½ cup finely chopped onion
1 tablespoon finely chopped raw mango
Salt and black pepper, to taste

FOR ASSEMBLY
10–15 papdis (page 174)
½ cup nylon sev
1 tablespoon finely chopped onion
Red chilli powder and cumin powder,
  as per taste

Method

1. Whisk the chilled thick yoghurt with orange juice, orange zest and salt. Refrigerate until needed.
2. **To make the lasagna mixture,** combine cottage cheese in a bowl with mashed potato, coriander leaves, mint leaves, and tamarind pulp. Add in red chilli and cumin powders, chaat masala, pomegranate gems, tomatoes, onions, and raw mango. Toss well and season to taste with salt and black pepper.
3. **To assemble,** create a layer of papdi at the bottom and spoon the lasagna mixture over it. Add another layer of papdi on top.
4. Pour the orange yoghurt over the papdi and garnish with sev, onion, red chilli powder and cumin powder. Set in the refrigerator for an hour and serve chilled.

UNIQUE CHAATS FROM MY KITCHEN 151

Quinoa and Olive Tikki Chaat

Olive cakes on a bed of quinoa

Time taken: 30 minutes | Serves 2

Ingredients

FOR THE OLIVE TIKKI
½ cup mashed cottage cheese
½ cup boiled and mashed potato
3 tablespoons grated cheese
2½ tablespoons finely chopped black olives
2 tablespoons finely chopped onion
2 teaspoons red chilli powder
2 teaspoons chaat masala (page 166)
½ teaspoon cumin powder
2 teaspoons garam masala
1 green chilli, finely chopped
2 tablespoons finely chopped coriander and mint leaves
2 teaspoons lemon juice
Salt, to taste
Sunflower or any neutral oil for frying
Breadcrumbs to roll

FOR THE QUINOA
1 cup boiled quinoa
1 tomato, very finely chopped
2 teaspoons finely chopped spring onions
2 tablespoons roasted sliced almonds, with skin
2 tablespoons olive oil
Salt, to taste
¼ cup finely chopped dried apricots
3 tablespoons crushed masala potato wafers
Juice of 1 lemon
2 tablespoons finely chopped fresh coriander leaves

Method

1. **To make the tikki**, combine the mashed cottage cheese and potato, grated cheese, black olives, and chopped onion in a bowl. Add the red chilli powder, chaat masala, cumin powder, garam masala, green chilli, coriander, and mint leaves. Add lemon juice over the mix and create a mixture using a potato masher. Taste and adjust the seasoning as needed
2. Heat the oil in a deep pan over medium heat.
3. Roll the mixture into 4 to 5 tikkis half the size of your palm and coat them with breadcrumbs. Deep fry them in batches until they are golden brown. Use a slotted spoon and drain on kitchen towels.
4. Toss the quinoa with chopped tomato and spring onion, sliced almonds, olive oil, and apricots. Season with a little salt.
5. **To serve,** create a bed of tossed quinoa on a serving plate and place the tikkis on top. Finish with crushed masala potato wafers, lemon juice, and coriander leaves.

UNIQUE CHAATS FROM MY KITCHEN 153

Burrata Papdi Chaat

Tangy tomatoes and crispy dough chips topped with burrata

Time taken: 30 minutes | Serves 4-6

Ingredients

FOR THE TOMATO CHAAT
½ cup yoghurt
1 tablespoon sugar
2 tablespoons ghee
1 teaspoon cumin seeds
1 teaspoon mustard seeds
1 pinch asafoetida
1 pinch black salt
3 teaspoons minced ginger
2 teaspoons minced green chilli
1 pinch deggi mirch powder (available at grocery stores)
1 cup finely chopped tomato
Salt, to taste
1 tablespoon finely chopped coriander leaves

TO ASSEMBLE
½ cup raw thinly sliced lotus root
Sunflower or any neutral oil for frying
3 large burrata
¼ cup tamarind–jaggery chutney (page 169)
¼ cup mint–coriander chutney (page 168)
12 papdis (page 174)
3 teaspoons chaat masala (page 166)

Method

1. Whisk the yoghurt and sugar until smooth. Set aside until needed.
2. Heat the ghee in a pan over medium heat and add cumin and mustard seeds. Add a pinch of asafoetida and black salt and cook until the seeds crackle.
3. Add the minced ginger and green chilli and sauté for a minute. Stir the deggi mirch powder into the masala followed by the chopped tomato. Mix well and cook until the tomato is soft.
4. Add a spoonful of tamarind–jaggery chutney and cook until the whole mixture becomes a soft mush. This should take about 4 to 5 minutes. Season to taste with salt and allow to cool. Add coriander leaves and set aside.
5. In another pan, deep fry the lotus root until golden brown and drain on kitchen towels. Sprinkle some salt and set aside.
6. **To serve,** use wide shallow bowls or plates for individual portions. Divide the tomato chaat into three equal parts.
7. Spoon the tomato chaat into the centre of the serving bowl and place a whole burrata on top. Arrange the papdi around the burrata. Drizzle the sweet yoghurt, tamarind–jaggery chutney, and mint–coriander chutney on the papdi and burrata.
8. Arrange the lotus root chips on each plate around the burrata chaat and finish with chaat masala.

BY CHEF MANISH MEHROTRA

UNIQUE CHAATS FROM MY KITCHEN 155

Ragda-Khari

Light, flaky biscuits topped with a white pea curry and chutneys

Time taken: 25 minutes | Serves 2-3

Ingredients

FOR THE RAGDA
1 tablespoon vegetable oil
2 teaspoons cumin seeds
1 pinch asafoetida
½ onion, finely chopped + 2 tablespoons for garnish
1 green chilli, finely chopped
2 teaspoons finely chopped garlic
1 tomato, finely chopped
½ teaspoon turmeric powder
1 teaspoon red chilli powder
½ cup boiled dried white peas
Salt, to taste

¼ cup yoghurt
½ tablespoon sugar
5-6 khari biscuits (available at grocery stores)
½ teaspoon grated raw mango
¼ cup date–tamarind chutney (page 168)
¼ cup green chilli–coriander chutney (page 170)
1 teaspoon chaat masala (page 166)
1 tablespoon finely chopped coriander leaves
Juice of ½ lemon
1 tablespoon sev

Method

1. Whisk the yoghurt and sugar until smooth. Set aside until needed.
2. **To make the ragda**, heat the oil and cumin seeds and a pinch of asafoetida in a pan over medium heat until they crackle. Add the onion, chilli, and garlic and cook for another minute. Add the finely chopped tomato and cook until soft (approximately 3 to 4 minutes).
3. Sprinkle the turmeric and red chilli powders over the masala and sauté for a few minutes over medium heat. Once the masala starts to soften, add the boiled peas and ¼ cup of water, gently smashing the peas into the mixture. Season to taste with salt. Mix once and set aside.
4. **To serve**, place the khari biscuits on a serving plate and spoon ragda onto each biscuit. Finish with raw mango, chutneys, chaat masala, sweetened yoghurt, coriander leaves, lemon juice, and sev.

8-Layered Dhokla Chaat

Each layer a burst of flavours and textures

Time taken: 30 minutes | Serves 4

Ingredients

LAYER 1 – MOONG
1 cup boiled green gram
¼ cup freshly grated coconut
1 teaspoon roasted cumin powder
1 teaspoon sugar
1 teaspoon chaat masala (page 166)
Salt, to taste

LAYER 2 – DHOKLA
1 teaspoon oil
½ teaspoon mustard seeds
1 teaspoon white sesame seeds
2 curry leaves
1 cup grated yellow dhokla
½ tablespoon chopped coriander leaves
Juice of ½ lemon
1 tablespoon nylon sev

LAYER 3 – POTATO
½ cup boiled and finely chopped potato
2 tablespoons grated beetroot
1 teaspoon red chilli powder
1 teaspoon chaat masala (page 166)
1 teaspoon dry mango powder
1 teaspoon roasted cumin powder
1 pinch turmeric powder

LAYER 4 – MATHRI
1 cup mathri (available at grocery stores)
½ cup finely chopped onion
½ cup finely chopped tomato
1 green chilli, finely chopped
½ teaspoon chaat masala (page 166)

LAYER 5 – CURD
½ cup hung curd
1 cup yoghurt
2 teaspoons red chilli powder
1 pinch dry mango powder
1 teaspoon sugar syrup or powdered sugar

LAYER 6 – MEETHA
1 tablespoon pomegranate gems
½ teaspoon sweet boondi (optional)

LAYER 7 – CHUTNEY
¼ cup green chilli–coriander chutney (page 170)
½ cup date–tamarind chutney (page 168)

LAYER 8 – GARNISH
1 tablespoon finely chopped coriander leaves
1 tablespoon finely chopped mint leaves
¼ teaspoon roasted and crushed fennel seeds

Method

1. Arrange your ingredients and bowls on the kitchen counter before starting.
2. **For layers 1, 3, 5, 6 and 8** use individual bowls and combine the ingredients for each. Set aside.
3. **To make the dhokla layer**, heat a teaspoon of oil in a pan and add the mustard seeds, sesame seeds, and curry leaves. Once they begin to crackle, add the grated dhokla and toss well in the tadka. Sprinkle with coriander leaves, lemon juice, and sev. Set aside.
4. **To make the mathri layer**, break the mathri into bite-sized pieces with your fingers. Toss in a bowl with the onions, tomatoes, green chilli, and chaat masala.
5. **To assemble**, you will need a deep, tall bowl or jar with a wide mouth. Layer the bottom of the jar with the green gram mixture, followed by the grated dhokla. Continue adding each layer to the jar in the order given.
6. Serve with a long spoon that can reach the bottom of the jar.

Tuscan Kale Chaat

Baked kale chips topped with veggies, yoghurt, and chutneys

Time taken: 25 minutes | Serves 4

Ingredients

1½ tablespoons olive oil
2 teaspoons chaat masala (page 166)
2 teaspoons red chilli powder
2 teaspoons roasted cumin powder
½ teaspoon dry mango powder
3 cups Tuscan kale leaves, washed and dried
1 onion, finely chopped
½ cup finely chopped tomato
¼ cup finely chopped potatoes, fried
½ cup whisked Greek yoghurt
3 tablespoons pomegranate gems
½ tablespoon boondi (salted)
Salt, to taste
2 tablespoons finely chopped coriander leaves
3 teaspoons honey

Method

1. Preheat the oven to 180 degrees C.
2. **To make the marinade,** combine the olive oil with 1 teaspoon each of chaat masala, red chilli and cumin powders, and dry mango powder in a bowl. Add a little salt and whisk.
3. Add the kale and rub the dressing onto the leaves for a few minutes.
4. Spread the kale on a baking sheet and bake in the oven for 10 to 12 minutes. Remove from the oven and allow the leaves to cool. The leaves will turn crisp, not black or dark.
5. Transfer the leaves onto a serving plate.
6. In a large bowl, toss together the finely chopped onions, tomatoes, fried potatoes, yoghurt, pomegranate gems and boondi, as well as the rest of the chaat masala, red chilli and cumin powders. Season to taste with salt.
7. Spoon the mixture onto each crisp kale leaf and finish with coriander leaves and honey.

UNIQUE CHAATS FROM MY KITCHEN 159

Avocado Taco Chaat
Indian-style healthy tacos

Time taken: 15 minutes | Serves 4

Ingredients
8 to 9 hard taco shells
1 cup finely cubed avocado
2 tablespoons finely chopped onion
2 tablespoons finely chopped tomato
2 tablespoons finely chopped cucumber
2 teaspoons finely chopped green chilli
1 teaspoon chaat masala (page 166)
1 teaspoon red chilli powder
1 teaspoon roasted cumin powder
Juice of 1 lemon
1 tablespoon roughly chopped roasted peanuts
2 tablespoons finely chopped coriander leaves
Salt, to taste
3 tablespoons mint–coriander chutney (page 168)
3 tablespoons date–tamarind chutney (page 168)
2 tablespoons nylon sev

Method
1. Arrange the taco shells on a serving platter and set aside.
2. Gently mix the diced avocado with onions, tomatoes, cucumber, green chilli, chaat masala, red chilli and cumin powders, lemon juice, peanuts, and coriander leaves.
3. Season liberally with salt.
4. Spoon the filling into taco shells and drizzle with mint–coriander chutney and date–tamarind chutney.
5. Finish with nylon sev and coriander leaves.

Guacamole Galauti
Avocado kebabs

Time taken: 25 minutes | Serves 4

Ingredients
1½ avocado, mashed
½ cup Bengal gram, boiled and mashed
3 teaspoons garam masala
2 red chillies, finely chopped
1 tablespoon lemon juice
1 tablespoon coriander powder
1 teaspoon mace powder
Pinch nutmeg
2 teaspoons cumin powder
¼ cup finely chopped coriander leaves
1 tablespoon corn flour
½ cup finely chopped onion
½ cup finely chopped tomato
½ cup grated parmesan cheese
Olive oil, for frying

TO SERVE
Homemade guacamole (page 174)
Sour cream
Salsa

Method
1. Combine the mashed avocado, boiled Bengal gram, garam masala, red chillies, lemon juice, coriander, mace, nutmeg and cumin powders, coriander leaves, and corn flour in a bowl. Mix until there is a thick mash. Add olive oil if needed.
2. Add the chopped onion and tomato to the mash and mix.
3. Next, add the grated cheese and combine well.
4. Roll the mixture into 4 to 5 small round patties and set aside.
5. Heat the olive oil in a pan over low heat. Shallow fry the patties in batches, until they are golden brown on both sides. Drain on kitchen towels.
6. Serve on a platter with guacamole, sour cream, and salsa.

UNIQUE CHAATS FROM MY KITCHEN 161

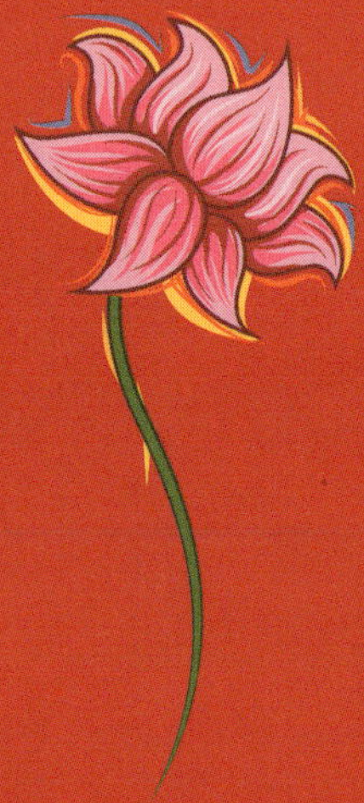

CHAAT MASALA, CHUTNEYS & DIPS

ALOO MASALA

TURMERIC

SPICY CURRY

GARAM MASALA

Chaat Masala

A spice mix that is the core flavouring of most chaat dishes in India

Time taken: 10 minutes

Ingredients
1 tablespoon cumin seeds
1 tablespoon coriander seeds
1 tablespoon carom seeds
1 teaspoon black peppercorns
1 tablespoon dry mango powder
¼ teaspoon dry ginger powder
½ teaspoon black salt
¼ teaspoon asafoetida

Method
1. Combine the cumin, coriander, carom seeds and peppercorns in a pan and place them over low heat. Dry roast the spices until they are fragrant. Set aside to cool. Place the cooled spices in a mixer-grinder and grind to a fine powder. Add the dry mango and ginger powders, black salt and asafoetida, and grind again. Store in an airtight jar.

Chaat Masala 2

A variation of the spice mix with added garam masala

Time taken: 10 minutes

Ingredients
2 tablespoons cumin seeds
2 dry Kashmiri red chillies
1 tablespoon black peppercorns
1 teaspoon dry ginger powder
1 tablespoon dry mango powder
1 tablespoon garam masala
½ tablespoon black salt
Salt, to taste

Method
1. Combine the cumin seeds, Kashmiri chillies and peppercorns in a pan and place them over low heat. Dry roast the spices until they are fragrant. Set aside to cool. Place the cooled spices in a mixer-grinder and grind until you have a fine powder. Add the dry ginger and mango powders, garam masala and black salt and blend again. Season to taste with salt and store in an airtight jar.

Chaat Masala 3

A variation of the spice mix with added citric acid and boriya chillies

Time taken: 15 minutes

Ingredients
¼ cup cumin seeds
½ cup coriander seeds
1 teaspoon sunflower or any neutral oil
1 cup boriya chillies
½ teaspoon citric acid
1 teaspoon black salt
½ teaspoon table salt

Method
1. Roast the cumin and coriander seeds in a pan for a few minutes over medium heat. Put the toasted spices into the jar of a mixer-grinder and put the pan back on the heat.
2. Heat the oil in the same pan and add the boriya chillies. Roast the chillies for a few minutes, making sure they don't darken. Add the roasted chillies to the cumin and coriander seeds in the mixer-grinder and grind into a fine powder. Add citric acid and salts and grind once again. Transfer the chaat masala in an airtight container and store.

Kala Chaat Masala

A unique black spice mix with notes of carom seeds and long pepper

Time taken: 15 minutes

Ingredients
7 dried red chillies
1 teaspoon carom seeds
3 tablespoons coriander seeds
½ cup cumin seeds
3 tablespoons black peppercorns
2 pieces long pepper
2 tablespoons dry mango powder
2 teaspoons dry ginger powder
Black salt, to taste

Method
1. Combine the red chillies, carom, coriander and cumin seeds, peppercorns, and long pepper in a pan and place them over low heat. Dry roast the spices for 3 to 4 minutes, turning up the heat in the end until the spices begin to release a gentle aroma. Set aside to cool. Place the cooled spices in a mixer-grinder and grind until you have a fine powder. Add the ginger powder and black salt and grind again. Use when needed.

CHAAT MASALA, CHUTNEYS & DIPS

Mint–Coriander Chutney

Classic Indian green chutney that is used in everything from chaats to sandwiches

Time taken: 10 minutes

Ingredients
1 cup fresh mint leaves
½ cup fresh coriander leaves
3 green chillies
1 teaspoon cumin seeds
1 teaspoon dry mango powder
2 tablespoons lemon juice
½ teaspoon sugar
5 tablespoons water
Salt, to taste

Method
1. Combine the mint and coriander leaves, green chillies and cumin seeds in a blender followed by dry mango powder, lemon juice, sugar, a pinch of salt, and water. Blend into a smooth thick paste, adding more water if necessary. Taste and adjust the salt. Refrigerate until ready to use.

Date–Tamarind Chutney

Classic Indian deep red chutney made of dates and tamarind

Time taken: 20 minutes

Ingredients
1 cup dates, seeded and finely chopped
½ cup tamarind, de-seeded
½ cup finely crumbled jaggery
½ cup water
1 teaspoon cumin powder
2 teaspoons red chilli powder
Salt, to taste

Method
1. Set a pan of water to boil over medium heat and add the finely chopped dates, tamarind, and crumbled jaggery. Mix well and allow it to come to a boil, approximately 3 to 4 minutes. Set aside to cool before blending into a smooth thick paste.
2. Strain the chutney through a fine sieve, discarding the molasses. Add the cumin and red chilli powders along with a pinch of salt and stir through. Refrigerate until ready to use.

Green Chilli–Garlic Chutney

A coarse chutney which promises only a spicy kick

Time taken: 10 minutes

Ingredients
4 green chillies
10 cloves of garlic
3 tbsp garlic chives (if in season)
3 tbsp roasted peanuts, skin removed and crushed
1 tsp cumin seeds
Salt, to taste
3 tbsp water
1 tbsp peanut oil

Method
1. In the small mixer-grinder jar, place the green chillies, garlic, roasted peanuts, and cumin seeds, and blend it into a coarse paste. Season to taste with salt.
2. Add water and oil, and blend again to obtain a slightly smoother paste.
3. The final chutney should not be very coarse, but not a smooth paste either. It should resemble a chunky tapenad.

Tamarind–Jaggery Chutney

A fresh fennel seed hinted sweet relish, aka saunth ki chutney

Time taken: 20 minutes

Ingredients
1 teaspoon sunflower or any neutral oil
1 teaspoon carom seeds
1 teaspoon fennel seeds
2 teaspoons dry ginger powder
2 teaspoons black pepper powder
1 teaspoon red chilli powder
¼ cup crumbled jaggery
½ cup tamarind pulp
2 teaspoons chaat masala
1 teaspoon black salt
⅓ cup water
Salt, to taste

Method
1. Heat the oil in a kadhai over medium heat and add the carom and fennel seeds. Once the seeds begin to crackle, add the dry ginger, black pepper and red chilli powders and mix well. Stir in the crumbled jaggery and tamarind pulp and continue cooking for 4 to 5 minutes, until it reduces by half. Sprinkle chaat masala and black salt and mix through. Slowly add hot water to the chutney, stirring continuously, until it is runny but not too thin. Season to taste with salt and serve when cool.

Red Garlic Chutney

Mildly hot Kashmiri chilli and garlic chutney

Time taken: 10 minutes

Ingredients
8 dry Kashmiri chillies, soaked in hot water for 20 minutes
2 teaspoons cumin powder
15 cloves garlic, peeled
½ tablespoon lemon juice
Salt, to taste

Method
1. Drain the water from the Kashmiri chillies and place them in a blender. Add the cumin powder, garlic cloves, lemon juice and a little salt and blend everything into a coarse paste. You may use a few drops of water if needed. Store the chutney in the refrigerator for up to three days.

Green Chilli–Coriander Chutney

Hari chutney

Time taken: 10 minutes

Ingredients
2 cups roughly chopped fresh coriander leaves
2 teaspoons roughly chopped green chillies
½ teaspoon cumin seeds
A pinch asafoetida
½ teaspoon coriander powder
Salt, to taste
½ teaspoon chaat masala (page 166)
1 teaspoon fresh lemon juice

Method
1. In a blender or chutney grinder, grind the coriander leaves, green chillies, cumin seeds, asafoetida, coriander powder, with 2 tablespoons of water to make a smooth paste. Season to taste with salt.
2. Transfer into a bowl and add the chaat masala and lemon juice.

Lemon Chutney

Whole lemon and spices relish

Time taken: 35 minutes

Ingredients
6 lemons, thoroughly washed
¼ cup white sugar
2 teaspoons sunflower or any neutral oil
1 teaspoon carom seeds
1 teaspoon fennel seeds
1 tablespoon red chilli powder
1 teaspoon cumin powder
1 tablespoon coriander powder
¼ cup lemon juice
Salt, to taste

Method
1. Bring a saucepan of water up to a rolling boil and add the whole lemons. Boil them until they are soft, approximately 12 to 15 minutes. Set aside to cool.
2. Cut each lemon into quarters and scoop out the flesh, placing it in a blender jar. Discard the seeds and skin. Add sugar and grind into a coarse paste.
3. Meanwhile, heat the oil in a small pan over medium heat and add the carom and fennel seeds. Once they begin to crackle, add the red chilli, cumin and coriander powders and stir well. Pour in the sweetened lemon paste and mix thoroughly. Add lemon juice and salt to taste. Serve immediately.

Sesame Seed Chutney

Sesame seed and split lentil paste, tempered with curry leaves

Time taken: 25 minutes

Ingredients
1 tablespoon sunflower or any neutral oil
2 dry red chillies
1½ tablespoons roasted white sesame seeds
1 tablespoon Bengal gram
½ tablespoon split black gram
1 pinch asafoetida
1 cup freshly grated coconut
1 tablespoon tamarind pulp
Salt, to taste

FOR TEMPERING
2 teaspoons sunflower or any neutral oil
8-9 curry leaves
1 teaspoon mustard seeds
2 teaspoons grated garlic

Method
1. Heat the oil in a pan over medium heat and add the red chilli, sesame seeds, Bengal gram, and split black gram. Add the asafoetida once the seeds begin to crackle. Stir in the freshly grated coconut and tamarind pulp and set aside to cool slightly. Transfer the mixture in a mixer-grinder and grind into a fine paste, adding a few tablespoons of water if needed.
2. **To make the tempering**, heat a little oil in the same pan over medium heat and add the curry leaves and mustard seeds. Add the grated garlic as soon as the seeds crackle and allow it to sputter. Pour on top of the chutney and serve.

Momo Chutney

A spicy garlic and chilli dip

Time taken: 10 minutes

Ingredients
2 tomatoes, boiled and roughly chopped
1 tablespoon tomato paste
5 dry red chillies
1 tablespoon roughly chopped garlic
1 teaspoon minced ginger
½ teaspoon black peppercorn
1 teaspoon soya sauce
½ teaspoon sugar
Salt, to taste

Method
1. Combine the tomatoes with the tomato paste in a blender followed by the chillies, garlic, ginger, and peppercorns. Add a teaspoon of soya sauce and a little sugar. Blend until smooth and season to taste with salt.
2. Strain the chutney and store in an airtight container and refrigerate for up to 3 days.

Kashmiri Doon Chetin

A radish, walnut and yoghurt dip

Time taken: 10 minutes

Ingredients
3 tablespoons grated radish
1 tablespoon roughly chopped mint leaves
½ cup peeled and halved walnuts
1 green chilli, roughly chopped
1 cup yoghurt
Salt, to taste

Method
1. Place the grated radish in the centre of a thin cloth and squeeze as much water out of it as you can. Set aside. Using a mortar and pestle, roughly grind the mint leaves, walnut halves, green chilli and some salt until it is a coarse mixture.
2. Spoon the yoghurt into a serving bowl and stir in the prepared mixture. Add the grated radish and combine, seasoning with salt as needed. This is best eaten fresh.

Besan Chutney

Chickpea flour and buttermilk based mild chutney

Time taken: 15 minutes

Ingredients
5 tablespoons chickpea flour
1 teaspoon red chilli powder
1 teaspoon black pepper powder
½ teaspoon turmeric powder
Salt, to taste
¾ cup buttermilk or water
1 tablespoon sunflower or any neutral oil
1 pinch asafoetida
5 curry leaves
1 green chilli, finely chopped
1 teaspoon mustard seeds
Juice of 1 lemon
1 tablespoon finely chopped coriander leaves

Method
1. In a bowl, combine the chickpea flour with red chilli, black pepper and turmeric powders. Season to taste with salt. Add either buttermilk or water and mix into a thick batter.
2. Heat the oil in a pan over medium heat and add the asafoetida, curry leaves, green chilli, and mustard seeds. Once the seeds begin to crackle, pour the chickpea batter into the pan and stir well. You may need to add a few tablespoons of water to get the consistency you want. Finish with lemon juice, fresh coriander leaves, and a sprinkle of salt. Serve warm.

Mullangi Thuvaiyal (Radish Chutney)

Grated radish chutney flavoured with fresh coconut and byadagi chillies

Time taken: 25 minutes

Ingredients
1 teaspoon sunflower or any neutral oil
1 tablespoon split white gram
1½ tablespoons split Bengal gram
5-6 fenugreek seeds
3 byadagi chillies
1 pinch asafoetida
¼ teaspoon turmeric powder
½ onion, thinly sliced
1 cup grated radish
Salt, to taste
1 tablespoon tamarind paste
3 teaspoon grated jaggery
3 tablespoons freshly grated coconut

FOR THE TEMPERING
1 tablespoon sunflower or any neutral oil
10 curry leaves
½ teaspoon mustard seeds
1 dry red chilli

Method
1. Heat the oil in a pan over medium heat and add the split white gram, Bengal gram, fenugreek seeds, byadagi chillies and asafoetida. Add the turmeric and mix well. Stir through thinly sliced onion and grated radish and sauté for 3 to 4 minutes, until the onions are translucent and the radish is cooked. Season to taste with salt, and add the tamarind paste and grated jaggery. Stir well and cook for another 2 minutes over low heat. Add the coconut and stir for another minute. Spoon the mixture into a serving bowl and set aside to cool.
2. **To make the tempering**, heat the oil in a small kadhai over medium heat. Add the curry leaves and mustard seeds. Once the leaves and seeds begin to crackle, add the dried red chilli. Pour the tempering over the stir fried onion and radish and serve fresh.

CHAAT MASALA, CHUTNEYS & DIPS

Papdi

This crispy flour cracker is a must-stock for anyone trying to make chaat

Time taken: 20 minutes

Ingredients
1 cup refined flour
½ teaspoon crushed fennel seeds
½ teaspoon crushed carom seeds
2 pinches salt
1 tablespoon sunflower or any neutral oil
Cold water to knead
Sunflower or neutral oil for frying

Method
1. In a wide bowl, combine the flour with fennel and carom seeds.
2. Add oil and salt and mix with your fingertips to get a rough, grainy texture.
3. Add water and knead into a firm, tight dough. Divide the dough into 5 roundels and roll each into a large sheet/roti of 10 mm thickness.
4. Using a sharp knife, make tiny incisions on the dough sheet, so the papdis do not puff while frying.
5. Using a circular cookie cutter (1½ inches), cut multiple small circles. Repeat the process on all dough sheets. This will make about 30–35 papdis.
6. Heat the oil in a kadhai over medium heat.
7. Working in batches, deep fry the papdis until golden brown and crisp. Use a slotted spoon and drain on kitchen towels. These can be stored in an airtight container for up to 2 weeks.

Guacamole

Classic Mexican dip

Time taken: 10 minutes

Ingredients
1 ripe avocado, finely chopped
Juice of ½ lemon
1 Serrano chilli (or jalapeño), de-seeded and finely chopped
¼ onion, finely chopped
½ tomato, finely chopped
2 tablespoon finely chopped fresh coriander leaves
Salt and black pepper, to taste

Method:
1. Place the chopped avocado in a medium-sized bowl and mash gently using a fork.
2. Add lemon juice and mix it once using a spoon so the avocado doesn't change colour.
3. Combine the chillies, onion, tomato, and coriander leaves to the avocado mash. Mix gently and season with salt and pepper.

Palak Chutney

Spinach and spices come together to create this dip

Time taken: 25 minutes

Ingredients
2 teaspoons sunflower or any neutral oil
1 teaspoon cumin seeds
½ teaspoon split black gram
½ teaspoon Bengal gram
1 teaspoon ginger-chilli paste
2 cups finely chopped spinach
1 cup freshly grated coconut
1 teaspoon grated jaggery
2 teaspoons tamarind paste
Salt, to taste

FOR TEMPERING
3 teaspoons sunflower or any neutral oil
¼ teaspoon mustard seeds
½ teaspoon split black gram
7-8 curry leaves
1 pinch asafoetida
1 dried red chilli

Method
1. Heat the oil in a pan over medium heat and add the cumin seeds, black gram and Bengal gram. Once the seeds begin to crackle, add the ginger and chilli paste and sauté for one minute. Tip in the chopped spinach with a little salt and continue to sauté until the spinach is cooked through. Set aside to cool before transferring to a blender. Add the grated coconut, jaggery and tamarind paste and blend into a thick paste.
2. **To make the tempering**, heat the oil in a small pan over medium heat and add the mustard seeds and black gram. Tip in the curry leaves and asafoetida. Once the leaves and seeds begin to crackle, add the dried red chilli. Pour the tempering over the spinach chutney and mix well.

Spicy Green Chilli and Peanut Chutney

A curry-leaf tempered peanut chutney

Time taken: 15 minutes

Ingredients
1 teaspoon sunflower or any neutral oil
2 teaspoons Bengal gram
8-10 curry leaves
1 tablespoon finely chopped garlic
3 green chillies, roughly chopped
2 tablespoons peanuts
1 cup finely chopped coriander leaves
5 tablespoons chopped mint leaves
1 tablespoon finely crumbled jaggery
1 tablespoon lemon juice
Salt, to taste

Method
1. Heat the oil in a pan over medium heat and add the Bengal gram, curry leaves, chopped garlic and green chilli along with peanuts. Cook until fragrant and set aside.
2. In the meantime, combine the coriander and mint leaves, jaggery and lemon juice in a blender, adding water until smooth. Pour the tempered spices into the chutney and blend once more, adding salt to taste. This chutney can be refrigerated for 2 to 3 days.

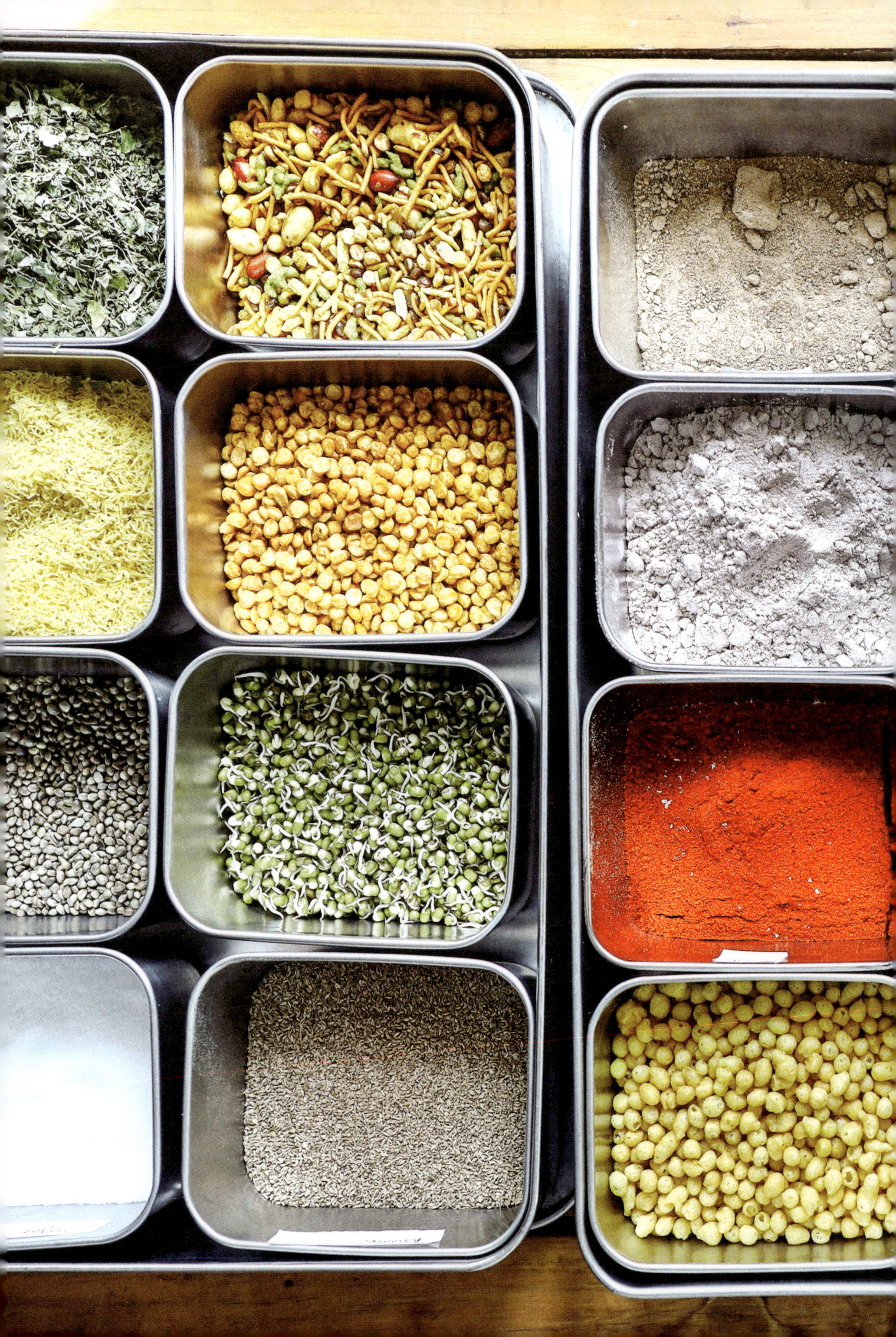

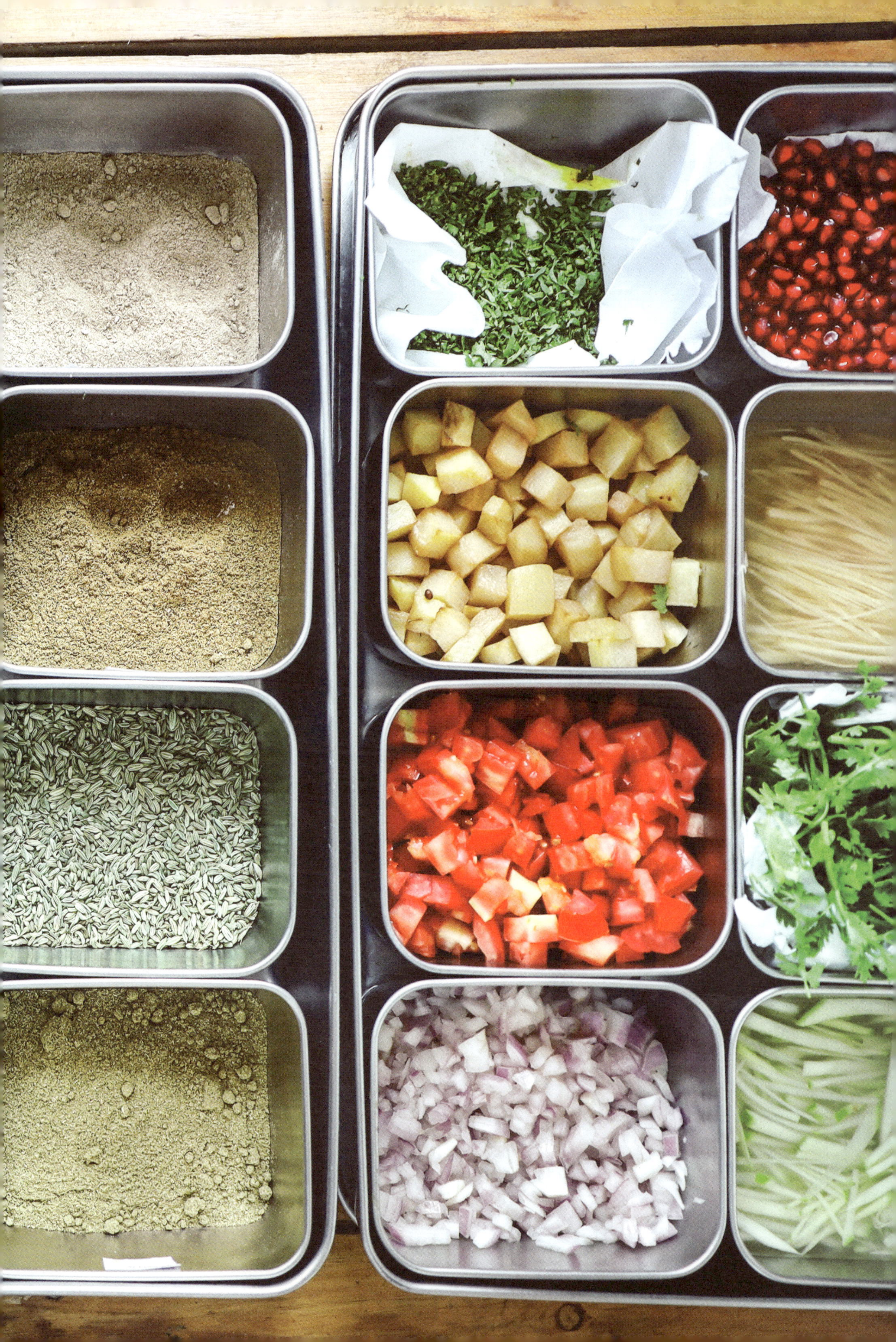

LEGENDS OF INDIA

Bazaars in cities and towns come alive in the evening with vendors selling street food that celebrates local flavours. Some of these shops selling your favourite chaats and street food are more than a hundred years old. Here is my list of iconic eateries from around India which offer food that is too delicious to miss.

AGRA

CHIMANLAL PURI WALE
One of the oldest restaurants in Agra, Chimanlal Puri Wale specializes in a UP speciality called bedmi puri and aloo ki subzi. The hot wheat puffs come filled with a thin line of spicy dal and are to be dunked in hot, rassewali subji that has plain potatoes with a surprise tanginess of pumpkin.

SARDAR BAZAAR
Agra's popular Chaat Gully is located in Sardar Bazaar with endless variations of Indian street food dishes such as a Schezwan frankie and a noodle dosa alongside the traditional Agra ki chaat. Take, for example, a Kurkuri Tikki Chaat stall that layers the tikkis with several kinds of chaat masalas with a hidden splattering of ginger shreds.

AHMEDABAD

DAS KHAMAN
With its humble beginnings on a pushcart in Ahmedabad in 1922, the award-winning Das Khaman is now a household name, serving the softest khaman and other Gujarati farsans (savouries) like patra and rice dhoklas.

JASUBEN SHAH OLD PIZZA
We would go here just to eat at one of India's most unique iterations of the good, old pizza. Jasuben's pizza has a base of soft pizza bread, topped with a spicy-sour tomato sauce and ample Amul cheese. This one isn't an exquisite pizza-eating experience, but turns the Italian dish into an outright Indian and Jain variation topped with mixed herbs and tomato sauce.

SHREE AMBIKA DALVADA CENTRE
You know the eatery is a hit when it simply focuses on doing one dish well. Dal vadas are lentil fritters served with chutney, raw onions and fried green chillies. This shop is known to make just this one dish and also packs you some raw batter to take a piece of them home.

ALLAHABAD

NIRALA KI CHAAT
An identification marker in the Loknath Lane, Nirala pays homage to the chaats of the country and remains one of the most popular places in Allahabad to do so. The dahi soonth ke bataashe and papdi chaat cannot be missed. They also serve the best milk concoctions like rabri, khurchan, and kulfi.

178   INDIA LOCAL

AMRITSAR

A-ONE KULFA
There is kulfi, plain and simple and then there is kulfa, the mother of all Indian ice cream inventions. A-One does a loaded kulfi that comes topped with all the items you'd find on a falooda, like the colourful seviyan, a massive dollop of rabdi and the dried fruits. This one's a filler!

DEEPAK CHAP CENTRE
Several soya nugget manufacturing factories in this city have given a rise to soya-based street snacks in Amritsar. This one tops the chart for their meat-free 'meaty' kebabs that come in coated marinations of spicy coriander-chilli, creamy cheese and yoghurt or tandoori masala.

MATHURA CHAT
For all those looking for a smacking snack after a long day of shopping in the city, Mathura Chat presents the burger redefined with an Indian twist – the simple aloo chaat and very glamorous bun tikki with an Indian-style potato patty packed inside a bun.

BANGALORE

ANAND
This wouldn't go into a list of street eats, but will definitely give you a sense of what Indian street style food is. Anand has been an iconic mithai shop in Bangalore for decades now. From mithais like kaju katli to boondi ladoo, to savouries like ready-to-eat chole bhature, dhokla sandwich and paneer tikka, everything you find at Anand is spot-on!

GANGOTREE
Running since 1986, Gangotree is one of the oldest chaat houses in town and contains nostalgia for many residents of Bangalore. They also have many dishes to please your sweet-tooth. Gangotree never disappoints when it comes to crowd-pleasing favourites like the papdi chaat, samosa chaat, and numerous sandwiches they offer.

GULLU'S CHAAT
If you're adventurous with your food, look no further than Gullu's Chaat in Seshadripuram. With innovative twists on classic chaats, their

speciality is the pizza pani puri, a puri stuffed with veggies and cheese. Also popular are the floating pani puri, bun nippat masala and, if you find yourself here in the summer, the mango bhel.

KARNATAKA BHEL HOUSE

Established in 1975, a tiny shop on the busy Bull Temple Road on Chamrajpet's Bazaar Street has now grown into a much larger albeit no-frills joint with limited seating. Famous for its authentic chaat, the masala puri and bhel puri here are unmissable.

RAMESHWARAM IDLI CAFE

Squarely in the middle of Bangalore's pub district, you can find the best podi idlis and other staple South Indian fare at this newer but already iconic cafe. Known to be crowded even at odd hours on the weekends, Rameshwaram Idli Cafe is making its mark on Bangalore's culinary scene with its trademark idlis and filtered coffee.

THINDI BEEDI (EAT STREET)

Located in VV Puram, this street is where all the Bangalore foodies go for anything and everything. Every evening, you can choose from traditional South Indian options like dosa, idli, paddu, holige apart from the usual street food fare of pav bhaji, dabeli, bhel puris as well as some new inventions like potato twisties.

DAVANGERE

SRI MANJUNATH MASALA MANDAKKI ANGADI

With several mills that produce mandakki (puffed rice) and the most delicious benne dosa, Davangare is worth the four-hour drive from Bangalore. At TS Manjunatha Masala Mandakki Angadi, the mandakki is stirred in with their famous masalas.

DELHI

BITTOO TIKKI WALA

In 1991, a small pushcart hawking aloo tikkis in Ranibagh in North Delhi has now turned into over 15 outlets in Delhi and a roaring catering business, serving all kinds of delectable chaats. It would be an injustice to your taste buds to deprive them of Bittoo Tikki Wala, AKA BTW.

GUPTA KANJI VADA

It's rare to find unique kanji vada being made on the street, but Gupta Kanji Vada comes as a savior. At this shop, you'll find not only kanji vada but also other cooling chaats such as dahi vada, papdi chaat and more.

HIRALAL CHAT CORNER

Over a century old, this iconic eatery rustles up some of the best aloo and fruit chaats in Old Delhi's Chawri Bazaar. Their beloved chaats illuminate the strong command that they have on flavour and spice.

JB KACHORIWALA

Another institution in Chandni Chowk, the award-winning Jung Bahadur Kachoriwala has been serving up hot, spicy urad dal kachoris since 1971 with their equally renowned kachalu chutney.

KHEMCHAND DAULAT KI CHAAT

On a pushcart in Old Delhi, come winter and you will find the Khemchand clan whipping up, quite literally, milk and cream to extract the lightest, creamiest, fluffiest foam, best known as Daulat ki Chaat, a special, labour-intensive treat.

NATRAJ DAHI BHALLA

Set up in 1940, Natraj Dahi Bhalla Corner is a small shop in Chandni Chowk marked by the large crowds found around it. Serving the fluffiest, creamiest dahi bhallas, the place also rustles up some terrific aloo tikkis.

SHYAM SWEETS

Established in 1910, Shyam Sweets is famous for its Desi Breakfast Platter consisting of a spicy potato bhaji, matar kachori, bedmi pooris, and chole. With its sweets no less popular, the shop in Old Delhi is best known for its Nagori halwa.

UPSC CHAAT WALA

Prabhu Chaat Bhandar in the UPSC lane is Delhi's chaat royalty, having been around for over 80 years now and the first in the chaat circuit to enter the income-tax bracket. Justifying the expression 'Don't judge a book by its cover', the unremarkable style of the stall is packed with crowds between 12 p.m. and 7 p.m., savouring its incomparable papdi chaat and other chaat offerings.

JAIPUR

RAWAT KI KACHORI

At this shop, you'll see cauldrons filled with floating hot stuffed kachoris. From a hole in the wall shop to a grand chaat shop, this is a must-visit! Rawat ki Kachori offers savoury options, in puris, and also sweet options like a sugar syrup-dunked mawa kachori.

JODHPUR

ARORA CHAAT BHANDAR

Spinach leaves coated in a chickpea flour batter deep-fried, topped with chutneys, chopped onions and tomatoes, chaat masala and thick yoghurt make up the most exceptional palak patta chaat that has elevated Arora Chaat Bhandar to the iconic institution that it is in Jodhpur today.

SHAHI SAMOSA

In 1984, the proprietor of this small stall looked out onto the Mehrangarh fort and decided to add a royal touch to the humble samosa by peppering it with some dry fruits. Now selling out over 10,000 samosas each day between 8 a.m. and 9 p.m, Shahi Samosa also packs a punch with its kachoris that hit the bull's eye and satisfy you each time.

GOA

SANDEEP GADDO

Sandeep Bhonsale's Gaddo Cart #37 is the last bastion of the food carts to stick around after the municipal crackdowns in Panjim where Sandeep is found every evening rustling up some delicious ros omelette. A popular street food delicacy in Goa, ros, means gravy in Konkani, usually a chicken or mutton xacuti masala gravy, into which an omelette is dunked and served with pav, onion, and lime.

VINAYAK FAMILY RESTAURANT

Another restaurant on our list that doesn't do traditional street food, but their offerings embody the vibe of tradition. In Goa, a trip without visiting Vinayak Family Restaurant is incomplete. They are popular for their fish thali, mackerel tossed in recheado sauce, fish fry, prawns curry and rice.

JOSHI DAHI BADA

With surprisingly affordable prices and flavourful food complimenting them, this eatery, on Safar Street, offers both outdoor and indoor seating. Visitors have a wide variety to choose from vada, chaat, and rolls to gulab jamun and yoghurt.

VIJAY CHAAT HOUSE

Bored of your usual aloo and ragda patties? This eatery has got your back! Offering their desperately craved khopra patties. Tikkis filled with spicy coconut stuffing are deep fried giving them the perfect crunchy texture. They come with a tangy red chutney, adding another layer of perfection.

KOLKATA

ANADI CABIN

The menu scribbled on the wall at this eatery is almost on the verge of erasure, but the flavours aren't. Anadi Cabin is known for Mughalai parottas, which are stuffed with meat, egg, chutneys and onions. They come neatly folded like an envelope, a cute square-shape, versus the traditional round or triangular Indian parathas.

K.C. DAS

One of the iconic sweet shops in Kolkata, you can get a street eat experience here by ordering a bunch of mithais served on a paper plate. Sitting in the shop, you'll finish the order faster than you can say kheer kodombo. The other big hits include roshogulla, sandesh, and saffron rasmalai. Another lesser recognized but deserving dish is radhaballavi, fried dal-stuffed puris.

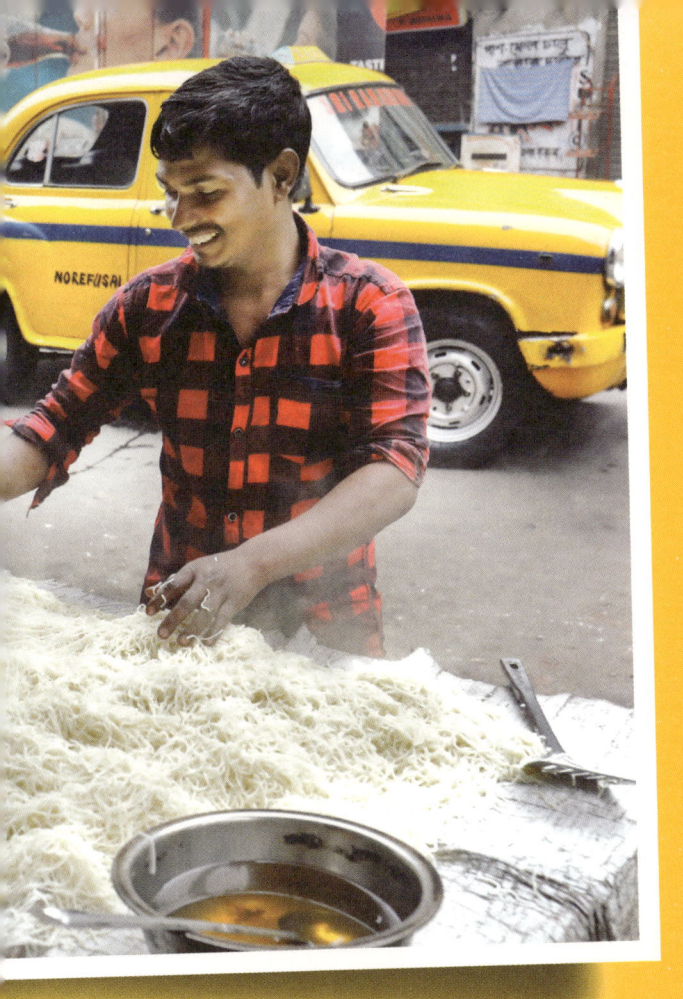

LUCKNOW

KING OF CHAAT
With a long history of adding taste to the streets of Lucknow, the regulars at King of Chaat repeatedly recommend the delicious aloo tikkis and spicy pani batashe, or gol gappe. Staying true to their name, they really are the kings of taste with their beloved papdi chaat and soft dahi badas.

BAJPAYEE KACHORI BHANDAR
This shop in Hazratganj entertains the crowd which starts gathering from 8 a.m. Some of the most popular dishes include their kachori sabzi, chole bhature, chicken and kulcha, balanced with a cup of tea.

MUMBAI

ASHOK VADA PAV
Time and again declared the best vada pav in Mumbai, no small feat for a stall in the city that consumes copious amounts of this iconic snack, this eatery has been around for over two decades, with regulars vouching for the unchanged taste of this vada pav stall outside Kirti College in Dadar.

BABULNATH DOSA CENTER
Right opposite the famous Babulnath temple in South Mumbai, the Babulnath Dosa Center grew from a street stall to a hole in the wall eatery. The most famous of their menu is the Mysore masala dosa that comes topped with ample cheese, a spice covered dosa sheet and a smackable garlic chutney.

BACHELORR'S
Nevermind the spelling of this eatery! Generations have seen this shop transform from a street stall into a full-fledged eatery that sells everything from the iconic Mumbai sandwich, cheese-loaded pizzas, and milkshakes galore. Regulars never leave without taking home the brain freezing chocolate milkshake.

KUSUM ROLLS
One of the most iconic kathi roll spots in Kolkata, Kusum Rolls makes rolls stuffed with egg, chicken and paneer. Through the years, the place has developed various varieties but the one dearest to the customers is still the original mutton roll. Their other rolls are loaded with cheese, mayonnaise, onion and fresh mint chutney that packs a serious punch.

LAXMI NARAYAN SHAW & SONS
Tel Bhaja, or fried veggies, cottage cheese and chops are what make this street stall unique. From eggplant fritters called beguni to vegetable and potato chop, to dhoka barfi (savoury treat that looks like dessert), this is one of the most unique street stalls you'll get your hands on.

SUBODH CHANDRA MULLICK
It's impossible to recommend a few dishes from this sweet shop's menu because nearly all of them are iconic but kheer kadam, a stuffed mithai, has to be the main character, followed by malai chum chum, gulab jamun, and kalakand.

BADSHAH FALOODA
Having been around since 1905, Badshah Falooda is one of the more iconic landmarks in the culinary landscape of Mumbai. The royal falooda at Badshah is unmatched in its flavour and texture. An Irani from Persia is credited for bringing Zoroastrian Persia's national drink, welcomed by the city with open arms.

CANNON PAV BHAJI
Originally meant to be a quick lunch for the textile workers in the many mills, pav bhaji is said to have originated over 170 years ago in Bombay. Extremely generous in their usage of butter, Cannon's standard pav bhaji is named for the eponymous brand of butter it uses, Amul. This place stays firm as one of the long-standing contenders for serving the best pav bhaji in the city.

ELCO
Since 1975, Elco in Bandra has been serving its iconic Indian street food dishes from tangy and cold pani puri, chaats like ragda pattice to its delicious dosas and creamy faloodas.

GURU KRIPA
What began in 1975 as a pushcart selling samosa and chole is today a restaurant and sweet shop in central Mumbai, recommended by everyone from Amitabh Bachchan to Chef Ranveer Brar. What remains unchanged is that Guru Kripa still serves the most delicious samosa chaat and chole puri in the city.

KALA GHODA'S SEV PURI
Right outside the FabIndia and Anita Dongre store at Kala Ghoda, sits a chaat shop that has been doing its thing for decades now. The word 'hygienic' is rarely said when street stalls are spoken of but Kala Ghoda's sev puri is one of the most hygienic street stalls in the city. You'll find sev puri and pani puri stuffed with hot ragda and cold water like no other.

JACKY BHEL PURI
In the 1960s when Mumbai was Bombay, in a by-lane in Juhu, a popular neighbourhood, best known for being home to the Hindi film industry's glitterati, a man hand-ground spices to mix into the chaats he served. Now known as Jacky Bhel Puri, this iconic stall still serves some of the best chaats in the city with Bollywood eating out of his hands.

MOTILAL GOLA
Icy frozen treats that are dosed in sugary syrup ranging from sweet red rose, black kala khatta, sour lime and sometimes even sweet Milkmaid and dried fruits are available at this moving cart to elevate your walks on Marine Drive every night. Motilal's gola cart has been going strong for over three decades.

PUDLA CENTER
A mixture of chickpea flour and mashed lentils is used to coat white bread. The bread is then pan-roasted like a savoury French toast, spiced and eaten with a range of chutneys. A pudla is a unique Gujarati dish that has found its own iteration in the streets of Mumbai.

MYSORE

USMAN DRY GOBI
For over twenty-five years, Usman of his namesake food stall has been serving just one dish in Mysore's chaat street outside Maharani College – the dry gobi (cauliflower) manchurian. Apparently even after making about a 100 kilos of the dish every day, it is not uncommon for Usman, the cook and owner, to run out before his usual closing time of 10 p.m.

NASIK

SHAUKIN BHEL
The famed makers of the jhatka bhel and pani puri, Shaukin Bhel began with just two dishes in 1999 – the regular pani puri and sev puri. Over the years, packed with several experiments, the two brothers at the little stall now serve many

variations of their classic chaats, leaning into the spicy Kolhapuri palette and guaranteeing their spot as the local favourite.

PUNE

BEDEKAR TEA STALL
Bedekar Tea Stall, a one-dish wonder in Pune, specializes in misal with a variety of breads and a Jain option to further excite you. You can also alternate your visits here with a plate of spicy potato vada (minus the bread) and kharvas, a sweet made out of coagulated milk.

GARDEN VADA PAV CENTER
Preserving Maharashtrian food specialties, Garden Vada Pav Centre is one of the oldest vada pav spots in the city. It offers a small menu with basic dishes to win over anyone who steps in their store. The most popular pick is the classic vada pav, misal pav, and buttermilk.

MAHALAXMI MISAL
With the crown owned by misal as the forerunner, this eatery gives a short menu, also serving puval and pav bhaji. However, nothing beats sol kadhi, a cool, refreshing drink on a hot afternoon made of coconut milk and kokum extract.

VAIDYA UPAHAR GRUHA
A rare delicacy called patal bhaji, a mixed potato gravy served with bread, finds home in this small eatery. Besides misal, which is this city's heart and soul, you can also opt for kanda poha, which is sweetened-caramelized onions tossed with flat rice.

VARANASI

RAM BHANDAR
In business since 1887, Ram Bhandar offers you the same taste and authenticity which made them famous years ago. With the foodies covering the narrow street it is situated in, many visitors start their mornings with their kachori, sabji, and jalebi.

DEENA CHAAT BHANDAR
This eatery offers a variety of taste palettes with their famed tamatar chaat, chuda matar, pani puri and dahi puri, falooda, and kulfi. One of the oldest chaat shops in the city of delectable flavours, this is equally popular with visitors as well as locals.

GLOSSARY

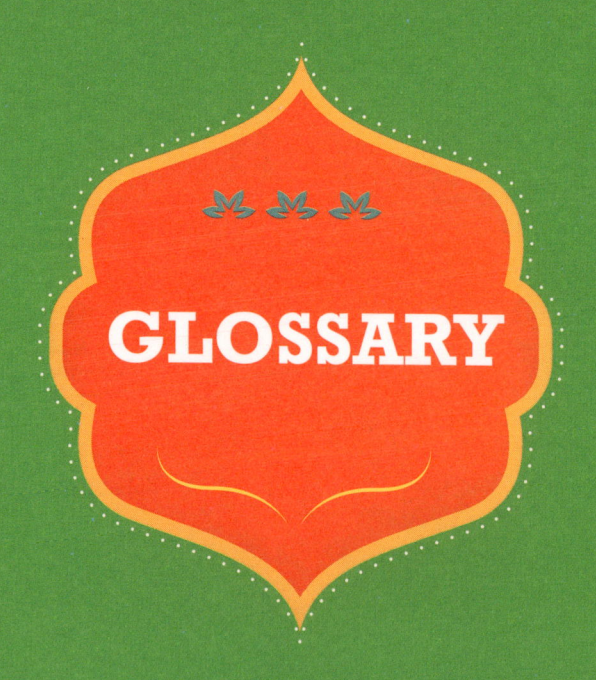

Alfalfa sprouts: Healthy and rich in vitamin C, these sprouts are also powerful antioxidants. They add texture and can be consumed in different ways.

Asafoetida (Hing): A type of resin added to dishes in minimal quantities to gently flavour the food. It is also known to have digestive benefits.

Bengal gram (Chana dal): One of the most basic pantry essentials, chana dal is split and polished in form. It is boiled to make curry, powdered to make chickpea flour or besan, and used in tempering.

Black gram (Urad Dal): A type of lentil that is commonly used in many dishes. They are usually small, black, dry beans and are available either split or skinned.

Black Salt (Kala Namak): Rich in minerals, this ingredient with a potent salty taste is used to flavour chaats, chutneys, and sherbets.

Boondi: Fried gram flour small-sized balls that are used as a garnish in chaats and to make boondi raita. Available in two varieties, salted and unsalted.

Bhavnagri chillies: Generally used for making stuffed chillies (bharwa mirch), this variety of chillies are relatively bigger and have a delicate peppery flavour. Considered less spicy, these come from Bhavnagar in Gujarat.

Boriya chillis: Large round chillis that are bright or dark red in colour. They are extremely spicy and are used in tadkas.

Cardamom (Elaichi): Available in green and black variety, elaichi is a true Indian superfood. Crushed or whole, they are added to Indian tempering.

Chickpea flour (Besan): This flour is made of powdered Bengal gram. It can be used as a coating or as batter for pakodas.

Cinnamon powder (Dalchini): A spice that is added for a rich aromatic touch to food. It is procured from the inner bark of the evergreen trees.

Couscous: This is a form of semolina granules but is slightly bigger.

Curry leaves (kadhi patta): These leaves form the backbone of a typical Indian tempering. It is used in abundance to flavour dry stir-fries, especially in South Indian cuisine. Sometimes, dried curry leaves are also powdered to make podi to sprinkle on dosas, idlis, and upmas.

Dry fenugreek leaves (Kasuri Methi): These dried leaves are used to finish several Indian delicacies. They have a distinct earthy aroma and flavour, which gets added to the dish they are sprinkled on.

Dry mango powder (Amchoor): Tart, sour notes to a dish can be added with a gentle splattering of dry mango powder. It is made by grinding dry pieces of mango. Amchoor is known to aid acidity and boost digestion.

Fafda: A popular Gujarati fried snack made with gram flour, turmeric and carom seeds.

Fennel seeds (Saunf): These seeds are added to dishes for their sprightly flavour. They are also eaten raw as a mouth-freshener.

Fenugreek seeds (Methi dana): These rough, coarse seeds from the methi or fenugreek plant are bitter but nutritious. They have high medicinal value, from helping with diabetes to acting as antioxidants. The seeds are soaked and blitzed into a paste or are used whole in tempering.

Green gram (Moong): This lentil can be either split or whole, and is usually soaked or boiled before use. It can be turned into a curry or fermented into a crepe.

Horse gram (Kala Chana): A fibrous lentil that is soaked and boiled before eating. A typical Indian way of eating it is to toss boiled kala chana with lemon juice, butter, coriander, chillies, and spices.

Jaggery (Gur): It is unrefined sugar, and a better alternative to common sugar. Gur can be mixed with water and turned into syrup.

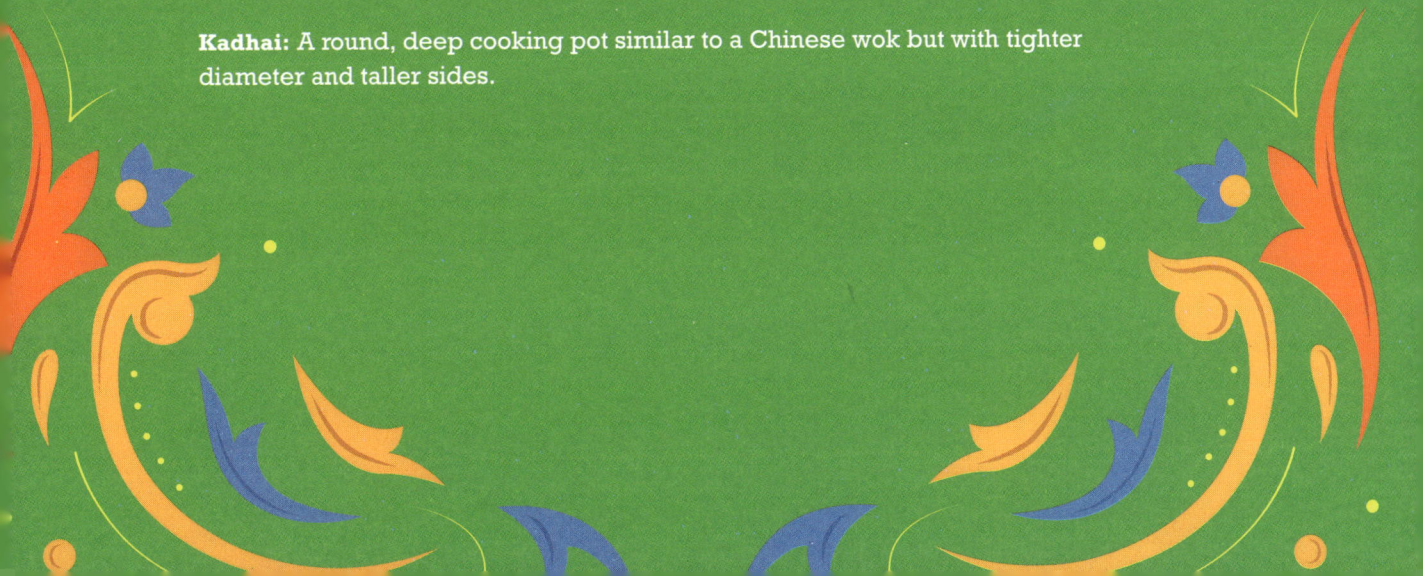

Kadhai: A round, deep cooking pot similar to a Chinese wok but with tighter diameter and taller sides.

Kolhapuri Chilli Powder: Finely ground, sun-dried red chilli peppers, this versatile spice is known for its bold, fiery flavour and rich, smoky aroma. The spice blend is named after the city of Kolhapur in Maharashtra, well known for its spicy cuisine.

Mathri: A flaky, crispy, deep fried North Indian snack. It is made with all-purpose flour and has a hint of spices and herbs.

Matki/moth or Turkish bean: Moth or Turkish bean is soaked in water overnight to enable it to sprout. The bean is boiled, tempered, and turned into a stir-fry or eaten as a salad.

Millets: Small seeded, whole grain cereal plants that are widely used in Asia and Africa. Different types of millet include Jowar, Bajra, Kangani, and Cheena.

Nylon Sev: An extremely fine-textured sev (made of fried gram flour) it resembles nylon threads.

Papdi: Crisp deep-fried Indian chaat snack made with whole wheat or refined flour.

Perilla seeds (Bhanjeera): A herb that belongs to the mint family. These seeds are aromatic and have a delicious nutty flavour. They are used as a spice and makes delicious chutneys and salads.

Poppy seeds (Khus Khus): A versatile ingredient known for its cooling properties, it is used in the form of a paste to add to various dishes, sweet and savoury.

Puffed rice (Kurmura): Made by heating rice kernels under high pressure in the presence of steam, Kurmura is used to make the most common and popular varieties of Indian snacks, called bhel.

Refined flour (Maida): Also known as all-purpose flour, maida is low in nutrition and is used to make a variety of breads and savouries.

Saffron (Kesar): One of the most expensive spices in India, saffron is used in sweet and savoury preparations to add a unique floral fragrance and flavour.

Semolina (Sooji/Rava): This can be used as coating or when mixed with milk and sugar can be used to make sweet dishes.

Sev: Very fine, vermicelli-like deep-fried noodles that are made with chickpea flour. They are thereafter broken into small pieces.

Split pigeon peas (Toor dal): This is the most common variety of lentil in the Indian pantry. It is usually boiled before use. Some recipes might call for soaking the dal in water overnight

Tamarind (Imli): This ingredient adds a sour, sweet taste to any dish it is added to. Available in pod form, it is usually pulped before use.

Tandoori masala: Is a mixture of spices for flavouring food cooked in a tandoor. With dominant flavours of cumin and coriander seeds, this masala is easily available in neighbourhood grocery stores.

Tava: A flat circular griddle used for cooking roti, dosa or parantha.

Tempura flour: Is a mixture of wheat flour and tapioca starch and is used to fry using less oil than traditional flour.

Turmeric leaves: Available in both fresh and dried forms, these aromatic leaves add a distinctive flavour to the food. They are commonly used in curries, soups, chutneys and as a wrapper for steamed dishes.

Tutti Frutti: Generally used for toppings in ice-cream, desserts or cakes, this is candied colourful confectionary made with fruits.

Vada/Vadai/Bada: A savoury fried snack made with ground green gram/black gram lentils.

White peas: These are also known as Navy Peas and are eaten when dried. They are healthy and rich in vitamins.

Whole-milk fudge (Khoya): A coarse, fudgy dairy product obtained by cooking milk until the liquid from it begins to evaporate. Khoya is sweetened with sugar or jaggery to turn it into a sweet dish.

Whole black gram (Sabut urad dal): This lentil resembles a black seed and is therefore known as black gram; it is also available in skinned form known as split black gram (dhuli urad). The latter is off-white in colour and is an excellent ingredient to ferment along with rice to make idlis, dosas, and other South Indian delicacies. The whole version is used to make creamy dals and curries.

Yellow peas: These are pale yellow or beige in colour and have a mild, slightly sweet flavour and a soft, granular texture.

INDEX

8 Layered Dhokla Chaat, 157

A

Aam Panna, 105
Alu Kachalu, 41
Amritsari Bun Chaat, 49
Amritsari Kulfa, 110
Amritsari Macchi, 118
Atho, 120
Avocado Taco Chaat, 160

B

Banarasi Tamatar Chaat, 52
Barley and Couscous Tikki,
    Mango Cream and Birista, 149
Besan Chutney, 173
Bhel
    Cheeseling Bhel, 53
    Chinese Bhel, 44
    Crispy Lamb Bhel, 86
    Geeli Bhel, 25
    Sukha Bhel, 28
    Vitamin Bhel, 54
Bhindi Bazaar Seekh Kebab, 134
Bihari Chaat, 47
Bihari Ghugni, 48
Bihari Kebab, 140
Bohri Samosa, 101
Bomb Batata, 42
Bombay Pav Bhaji, 115
Bombay Sandwich, 124
Bread/Bun
    Amritsari Bun Chaat, 49

Bombay Pav Bhaji, 115
Bombay Sandwich, 124
Bun Maska, 100
Bun Maska, 100
Burrata Papdi Chaat, 154
Butter Sada Dosa, 94

C

Chaat
    8-Layered Dhokla Chaat, 157
    Amritsari Bun Chaat, 49
    Avocado Taco Chaat, 160
    Banarasi Tamatar Chaat, 52
    Bihari Chaat, 47
    Cheesy Paneer Cone
        Chaat, 146
    Chicken Chaat, 84
    Chole Chaat, 67
    Creamy Aloo Chaat, 40
    Dahi Papdi Chaat, 32
    Daulat Ki Chaat, 100
    Dhakai Chaat, 33
    Karari Aloo Tikki Chaat with
        Peas Filling, 38
    Fafda Chaat, 72
    Healthy Moth Ki Chaat, 56
    Indore Namkeen Chaat, 53
    Jacket Potato Chaat, 78
    Kala Chana Chaat, 60
    Kand Tikki Chaat, 80
    Karari Bhindi Chaat, 81
    Kolhapuri Bhadang Chaat, 46
    Kulle Ki Chaat, 61
    Palak Patta Chaat, 73

    Peanut Chaat, 58
    Quinoa and Olive tikki
        Chaat, 152
    Samosa Chaat, 70
    Surti Corn Chaat, 34
    Sweet Potato Tikki Chaat, 57
    Tawa Paneer Chaat, 62
    Tokri Chaat, 68
    Tulsi-Cinnamon Fruit Chaat, 58
    Tuscan Kale Chaat, 158
Chaat Masala, 166
Chaat Masala 2, 166
Chaat Masala 3, 167
Cheeseling Bhel, 53
Cheesy Paneer Cone Chaat, 146
Chicken
    Bihari Kebab, 140
    Chicken Chaat, 84
    Chicken Shawarma, 136
    Kolkata Kathi Roll, 127
Chicken Chaat, 84
Chicken Shawarma, 136
Chickpeas
    Chole Chaat, 67
    Kala Chana Chaat, 60
    Ragda Patties, 71
    Samosa Chaat, 70
    Sundal, 118
Chinese Bhel, 44
Chole Chaat, 67
Chutney
    Besan Chutney, 173
    Date-Tamarind Chutney, 168
    Green Chilli-Coriander
        Chutney, 170

Green Chilli-Garlic Chutney, 169
Kashmiri Doon Chetin, 172
Lemon Chutney, 171
Mint-Coriander Chutney, 168
Momo Chutney, 172
Mullangi Thuviayal (Radish Chutney), 173
Palak Chutney, 175
Red Garlic Chutney, 170
Sesame Seed Chutney, 171
Spicy Green Chilli and Peanut Chutney, 175
Tamarind-Jaggery Chutney, 169
Classic Sev Puri, 26
Creamy Aloo Chaat, 40
Crispy Lamb Bhel, 86
Cutting Chai, 102

D

Dahi Bhalle, 30
Dahi Gujiya, 31
Dahi Papdi Chaat, 32
Dakor Na Gota, 123
Date-Tamarind Chutney, 169
Daulat Ki Chaat, 100
Dhakai Chaat, 33
Dosa
   Butter Sada Dosa, 94
   Jinni Dosa, 96

E

Egg
   Egg Banjo, 131
   Egg Tikka, 132
Muttai Kalaki, 140
Egg Banjo, 131
Egg Tikka, 132

F

Fafda Chaat, 72
Faraal Sev Puri, 24
Frankie, 108

G

Geeli Bhel, 25
Green Chilli-Coriander Chutney, 170
Green Chilli-Garlic Chutney, 169

Guacamole, 174
Guacamole Galauti, 160

H

Healthy Moth Ki Chaat, 56
Indore Namkeen Chaat, 53

I

Indori Kees, 102

J

Jacket Potato Chaat, 78
Jil Jil Jigarthanda, 106
Jinni Dosa, 96

K

Kala Chaat Masala, 167
Kala Chana Chaat, 60
Kand Tikki Chaat, 80
Kanda Bhajiya, 116
Kanji Vada, 74
Karari Aloo Tikki Chaat with Peas Filling, 38
Karari Bhindi Chaat, 81
Kashmiri Doon Chetin, 172
Kashmiri Kahwa, 104
Kashmiri Masalah Tchot, 112
Kashmiri Mutton Tujj, 128
Kebab
   Bhindi Bazaar Seekh Kebab, 134
   Bihari Kebab, 140
   Guacamole Galauti, 160
Keema Baida Roti, 141
Khopra Pattice, 114
Kolhapuri Bhadang Chaat, 46
Kolkata Kathi Roll, 127
Kothambir Vadi, 97
Kulle Ki Chaat, 61
Kumaoni Bada, 126

L

Lal Aloo Wai Wai, 98
Lemon Chutney, 171

M

Mango Lassi, 104
Manipuri Singju, 94
Mint-Coriander Chutney, 168

Momo Chutney, 172
Mountain Maggi, 120
Muttai Kalaki, 140
Mutton
   Bhindi Bazaar Seekh Kebab, 134
   Bohri Samosa, 101
   Crispy Lamb Bhel, 86
   Kashmiri Mutton Tujj, 128
   Keema Baida Roti, 141
   Mutton Momos, 137
   Sha Phaley, 138
Mutton Momos, 137

N

Nimki Makha, 77
Noodles
   Atho, 120
   Chinese Bhel, 44
   Lal Aloo Wai Wai, 98
   Mountain Maggi, 120
   Thukpa, 106

P

Paknam, 130
Palak Chutney, 175
Palak Patta Chaat, 73
Paneer
   Cheesy Paneer Cone Chaat, 146
   Paneer Dahi Vada, 36
   Paneer Tikka, 126
   Tawa Paneer Chaat, 62
Paneer Dahi Vada, 36
Paneer Tikka, 126
Pani Puri, 82
Pani Puri with Asian slaw and Fragrant Herb Water, 148
Papdi, 174
Papdi 'Lasagna' with Orange Yoghurt, 150
Peanut Chaat, 58
Potato
   Alu Kachalu, 41
   Amritsari Bun Chaat, 49
   Barley and Couscous Tikki, 149
   Mango Cream and Birista, 149
   Bihari Chaat, 47
   Bomb Batata, 42
   Bombay Pav Bhaji, 115
   Bombay Sandwich, 124
   Cheeseling Bhel, 53
   Classic Sev Puri, 26

Creamy Aloo Chaat, 40
Crispy Lamb Bhel, 86
Dahi Papdi Chaat, 32
Dhakai Chaat, 33
Fafda Chaat, 72
Faraal Sev Puri, 77
Frankie, 108
Geeli Bhel, 25
Healthy Moth Ki Chaat, 56
Indore Namkeen Chaat, 53
Jacket Potato Chaat, 78
Kala Chana Chaat, 60
Karari Aloo Tikki Chaat with Peas Filling, 38
Khopra Pattice, 114
Lal Aloo Wai Wai, 98
Paneer Dahi Vada, 36
Pani Puri, 82
Papdi 'Lasagna' with Orange Yoghurt, 150
Peanut Chaat, 58
Pyaaz Ki Kachori, 66
Quinoa and Olive Tikki Chaat, 152
Ragda-Khari, 156
Ragda Patties, 71
Railway Cutlet, 116
Raj Kachori, 64
Rajasthani Mirchi Vada, 50
Samosa Chaat, 70
Sukha Bhel, 28
Sukha Puri with Aloo, 34
Tokri Chaat, 68
Tuscan Kale Chaat, 158
Vada Pav, 122
Pyaaz Ki Kachori, 66

Q

Quinoa and Olive Tikki Chaat, 152

R

Ragda Patties, 71
Ragda-Khari, 156
Railway Cutlet, 116
Raj Kachori, 64
Rajasthani Mirchi Vada, 50
Ram Ladoo, 76
Red Garlic Chutney, 170

S

Samosa Chaat, 70
Sel Roti, 114
Sesame Seed Chutney, 171
Sha Phaley, 138
Shikanji, 105
Sindhi Dal Pakwan, 92
Spicy Green Chilli and Peanut Chutney, 175
Sukha Bhel, 28
Sukha Puri with Aloo, 34
Sundal, 118
Surti Corn Chaat, 34
Sweet Potato Tikki Chaat, 57

T

Tamarind-Jaggery Chutney, 169
Tawa Paneer Chaat, 62
Thair Vadais, 109
Tender Coconut Shake, 123
Thukpa, 106
Tikki
   Barley and Couscous Tikki, Mango Cream and Birista, 149
   Kand Tikki Chaat, 80
   Karari Aloo Tikki Chaat with Peas Filling, 38
   Quinoa and Olive Tikki, 152
   Sweet Potato Tikki Chaat, 57
Tokri Chaat, 68
Tulsi-Cinnamon Fruit Chaat, 58
Tuscan Kale Chaat, 158

V

Vada Pav, 122
Vitamin Bhel, 54

Y

Yoghurt
   Dahi Bhalle, 30
   Dahi Gujiya, 31
   Dahi Papdi Chaat, 32
   Paneer Dahi Vada, 36
   Papdi 'Lasagna' with Orange Yoghurt, 150
   Thair Vadais, 109